Tax-Free Retirement

Patrick Kelly
© 2007

Note for Librarians: A cataloguing record for this book is available from Library and Archives Canada at www.collectionscanada.ca/amicus/index-e.html

ISBN 1-4251-1082-7

Printed in China

What agents are saying about Tax-Free Retirement...

"I've read this book. It is a great book. It puts in writing what we've preached at Kinder Brothers for 30 years. Get this book into the hands of all your clients!"

"Patrick has the uncanny ability to take a complicated idea and make it simple and easy to understand for both the practitioner as well as the layman. This is the best book I have ever read that covers this subject so thoroughly."

"Wow!!!! I stayed up until 3 a.m. to finish Patrick's book. I just couldn't put it down. This is a concept perfectly articulated in simple terms. Put in an order for 100 copies for me."

"I've been in the business since 1964 and this is by far the best book regarding life insurance that I have ever seen. Great ideas written with such simplicity and clarity that even our clients and prospects will have no trouble comprehending. I have ordered many copies for my clients and it has been enthusiastically received. Congratulations!"

"Not only is this book a practical guide for the consumer to make wise financial decisions, but it is also a must read for the financial professional!"

"WOW!!! I just finished the book and have been sitting here for the last thirty minutes or so thinking about the impact the concepts you have brought to light will have on the thousands of people you will undoubtedly touch either directly or indirectly. In my own family this will set a new direction and way of thinking for the remainder of the accumulation phase of our planning. In the distribution phase we will have options that would not have been considered and we will have the opportunity to touch so many with so much more. Thank you."

"Amazingly easy to read and understand. Once I started reading I could not put it down. I ordered 10 books to immediately give to my clients. Thank you for making the principles in your book easy to understand."

"Patrick's easy-to-understand way of explaining things has given my clients a greater sense of clarity and the little extra nudge needed to take positive action for their future."

"Patrick has taken concepts that are increasingly being used by progressive financial services experts and extrapolated them into a language easily understood by the masses. I can't wait to get this book into the hands of my high-income, high-net-worth clients. If they can grasp the concepts laid out in this book, I believe it will have a profoundly positive impact for their futures."

"Patrick, what a great book!! Your writing is very entertaining and I love the way the anticipation builds so that I couldn't wait to get to the end of the book."

"How many books on retirement planning and financial planning are so interesting you can't put them down? This is one of the few. Patrick's book not only outlines some of the mistakes people often make with their money, but presents in a simple way an alternative to retirement planning that many people are not aware of. I know both financial professionals and their clients would benefit from the ideas presented in his book"

"Patrick's book was a REAL eye-opener. I finally have a full grasp of the incredible magnitude of the LIVING BENEFITS offered by Universal Life insurance. Much more important, though, anyone can read his book and have a clear understanding of and appreciation for the true value of Universal Life. Now, I consider it my personal responsibility to share this treasure with all my higher-income clients because I can make a difference in their lives."

"Patrick has a knack for putting money concepts into words that make sense. He clarifies strategies, so they seem achievable, and the message is effective for clients at any level in their financial planning. Clients' eyes are opening to the options and possibilities they have for their future."

"Patrick's book was incredibly clear and concise. It was an enjoyable read and I found myself nodding in agreement from beginning to end. This book has helped me spend my time with only qualified prospects who are ready to move forward."

"Loved your book! It was a quick, easy read, and very understandable."

"Patrick's ideas and concepts are both easy to understand and easy to use. This is a very quick read with an abundance of practical tools to benefit any individual in their financial planning."

"Patrick's down to earth practical insights will enlighten you to make changes in your retirement planning strategies. The outcome will maximize your standard of living in your golden years, while protecting the ones you love most!"

"Outliving one's money is the number one fear of the senior community. Your book supplies the answers on how to stretch those dollars to the max. Thank you for showing us how we can help others live a more secure and better life."

"Wow! What a smooth, easy read. I felt like I was reading my own words. Your metaphors and stories are right on, accurate, and to the point. When you publish this, I'll take 50 copies."

"LOVE your book. It was like a bowl of M&M's®. Once I started I couldn't stop until I had eaten the whole bowl."

"Patrick's book is a very easy read. My copies are now in the hands of my team and my clients. The concept is easy to understand and very practical. Thank you!"

"Your book is wonderful! I have my husband reading it next."

This book is dedicated to my four children – Caryn, Brett, Rylan and Aubrey – may God grant you the ability to dream big dreams, the compassion to walk in the footsteps of those less fortunate, and the desire to make a positive impact in the lives of many.

I love each of you very much!

Table of Contents

Part IV: The Retirement Solution

Part V: Individual Applications

Part VI: The Next Step

<u>Acknowledgments</u>

I'd like to thank the many individuals who assisted and encouraged me during this project – please know that this is a better book because of your contribution.

To the many insurance agents all over the country who took the time to read the manuscript in its many developing stages, your honest feedback was invaluable.

To those of you who endorsed this book, I am humbled by your comments.

To my wonderful and talented team, your encouragement kept me going; without you the book may have never made it to the publisher.

To Art Moore, for employing his sharply trained editor's eye; it's amazing what you can see.

To Ricky Russ, your cover design is a work of art, and more than I could have hoped for.

And to my all-time favorite editor and friend, Marly; without you our kids would die of scurvy, and my writing would be unworthy of print. You inspire me!

Preface

I've heard it said that having children is a bit like having your heart walk around outside your body. Publishing a book feels much the same. It's a weighty and intimidating prospect. Yet the pain of childbirth (not that I know first-hand) is soon replaced by a fresh exhilaration, as the child takes on a life of his own. Likewise, the weightiness of this project has been far overshadowed by the excitement of the finished product, and the hope I have for this book to transform your life, and the lives of countless individuals around the globe, many of whom will never read it, but simply be the benefactor of a generous spirit and your willingness to make a difference.

This book has been over a decade in the making – from life experience, to formulative idea, to written word, to finished product. It has taken shape in stages, with many fits and starts, much like the diverse phases of a child's development. And let me tell you, this book spent much of its existence in a prolonged and disorderly adolescence.

It is extremely important to me that you know my intentions for this book. If I were not to share those with you specifically, you would be left to make inferences, which always opens the door to grave misunderstandings. (Any of you who are married know what I mean.)

My hope for this book is singular in focus – I want it to make a positive difference in your life. Yet, that narrow aim has three equally significant components:

- First, I hope this book helps you manage all the aspects of your finances – including saving, debt-management, and retirement-planning – with a new-found freedom and enthusiasm.

- Second, I want you to understand a time-tested, yet startlingly unknown plan to accumulate long-term savings that can minimize the severe impact of future taxes.
- Third, and most importantly, I hope this book propels you to *use* this new-found knowledge to maximize your wealth for the benefit of the hurting and needy around the world.

If this book comes even close to achieving these ends, I will count my years working on it well-spent.

I also want to share what this book is *not*. This is *not* a get-rich-quick plan. This is *not* a radical new idea. And this is *not* a promise of great wealth. As a matter of fact, this book does not promise anything, except to provide a few hours of reading.

On that same topic, the illustrations in this book are purely conceptual in nature. They are intended to expand your financial knowledge, not to provide you with any type of personal or investment instruction. While the concepts can work beautifully if managed properly, even the best plan can be grossly mismanaged and turn out a complete disaster. It all depends on wise choices and proper execution.

Also, as obvious as this may sound, this book was written in the present, *not* the future. While the concepts in it worked the day it was written, I make no promise that they will continue to be true in the future. While it is my *hope* that these concepts will stand the test of time, tax laws are continually altered to meet the changing needs of our society and economy. So, once again, this book is simply intended to move you in the right direction; a direction that finds you seeking advice from a qualified professional, who can guide you along through the years in a well-managed and capable fashion.

As I close, I must say, I feel a bit like a river-rafting guide, elated to share the unique scenery of my river, yet anxious about helping you navigate the turbulent white-water you will undoubtedly experience. So with that final picture, I hereby declare, "Welcome to the adventure!"

Part I: The Foundation

1

How it All Started

We live in a world of financial noise. Everywhere we turn we are being bombarded by gimmicks and scams. Today's financial media cloaks itself as providing reliable, useful information when actually it is nothing more than financial entertainment. It's unreliable. It's passé. It's old news by the time it airs on television.

There is no better example in recent history than the technology stock boom and crash. People who had never before purchased a stock were now giving stock tips. Where did they get their reliable information? From financial television shows and Internet chat rooms. Complete neophytes were donned with guru status overnight by giving one hot pick, one great insight. Newsletters were written. Web sites were created. Heroes were born.

However, the public was duped. Fortunes were lost. Untold wealth dwindled to nothing. Mansions were foreclosed upon. Luxury cars were repossessed. And for many Americans, retirements were delayed. We all know this now, for hindsight is 20/20.

People were driven by greed. They all wanted their share. No one wanted to miss out on the next Microsoft, Netscape, or AOL.

The financial tide was rising and all ships were being lifted. But, you never know who is swimming naked until the tide goes out. As it was, there was a lot of financial skinny dipping going on. People were trapped, afraid to get out of the water. So what did they do? They rode the tide all the way down, down to the very bottom, until there was nothing left but dry bank accounts and horrific margin calls.

How do I know this? I was one of those financial skinny dippers. Though not a true day trader, I was buying and selling stocks every week. I was buying companies I had no right to buy, with money I had no right to invest, on tips from individuals who had no right to be listened to. Ironically, the worst tips and my largest mistakes came from "professional" stock brokers. What I realized was that they didn't know any more than I did. And in many ways they knew less. If I had followed my own plan, my investment account would have been in the seven-digit range, even after the tech crash. Instead, it was vaporized. What I soon realized was that many stock brokers were simply puppets for their company's analysts; and the analysts were motivated by their own greed and underwriting ventures. It was self-serving manipulation disguised as financial wisdom.

During a five-year period I made a lot of money, and in a few short months and a few poor decisions, I lost it all.

My next statement may seem odd to you now, but it will be crystal clear by the time you are done with this book. This event was one of the greatest experiences of my entire life. Though my investment accounts were hemorrhaging, I had received a far greater prize ... a PhD in life. I had gained wisdom both in and beyond the financial realm. And most importantly, I was ready to do things differently. To find a plan that would win for the long run. Not a get-rich-quick scheme, the next hot stock, or some new financial fad, but a tried-and-true investment strategy that would win the game for decades down the road.

My quest had begun.

Before I walk you along the path of my journey, I think it's important that you have a little understanding of my background. I have been a licensed insurance agent with a major U.S. corporation for fifteen years. During these years I have served different roles within the company. I have also seen major changes to the insurance and financial landscape. I began my agency career with this company in Seattle, Washington. As a new agent, I had been married two years and was expecting our first child. Life was good and business was predictable. At that time, the company I represented had all the day to day insurance products available… auto, home, business, life, and some health insurance.

After three years, predictability turned to boredom. Business was growing, but it had lost my interest. I remember driving home one evening and laughing out loud to myself in the car as I spoke an audible thought, "God, you are going to have to do a miracle to keep me in this job for thirty years."

My restlessness forced me to venture out to look for other avenues for my energies. This was when I discovered stocks. It was 1994. I began trading long before it was the trendy thing to do. I ventured next into commodities. I spent hours each night learning the ins and outs of the financial world. I was having a blast and making money … a lot of money.

About this same time, I was asked by my company to join their agency management team as a consultant down in Tacoma, Washington. It seemed like a perfect fit for my restlessness and would allow me to fulfill a long-time dream of living in a quaint harbor town that served as a bedroom community for the Tacoma business market. I accepted.

Since my financial research was done in the evenings on my personal time, I was able to accommodate my new position within the company as well as my financial undertakings. I was enjoying both and finding equal success in each.

One unique feature about corporate America, however, is its propensity to move employees. After six years in management, it was clear that the next move was looming on the horizon. Conversations were underway. Options were being laid out. The next step was still to be seen, but one thing was clear – it would be a long way from our quaint little waterfront town. I was torn. I loved my career as well as the prospect of living in different parts of the country. However, our family of three had grown to a family of five. We had connections in the community, and the desire to plant deep roots won over the desire for career adventure.

So, in a miraculous way, I found myself back in personal production as an insurance agent in January 2001. But everything had changed. The financial landscape had been transformed. Insurance companies were offering bank products and banks were selling insurance. Everybody was in everybody else's business. It was now one financial marketplace, and I was ready to dive in.

I was ready to build wealth a new way. However, I didn't yet know what that meant. I was going to make an honest search unlike any I had ever made before. I wasn't going to settle for an answer just because someone told me it was good. I was going to do my own homework … flesh out the real data. Every last detail had to make financial sense. Other than individual stocks and commodities, at that time, I was able to sell most other financial products. I could offer 401(k) plans, SEPs, Roth IRAs, Traditional IRAs, and personally designed pension and profit-sharing plans. And I could fund these plans with a bucket-load of different products. I had just about everything in my own arsenal of products.

However, I was willing to go outside of my own business if necessary in order to find the best plan to build consistent wealth for the long-term; and because of my financial endeavors, I had the knowledge base to know where to find it.

I wiped the slate clean of all my preconceived beliefs and was willing to give each plan and strategy an equal and fair shot at victory. I wanted to pursue an honest search in which the winner was proclaimed by the facts, not by emotional attachment or personal access to a particular product.

The result of the search was shocking. If you would have laid a million dollars on a table in front of me and told me that all the money would be mine if I could name the product that would become the eventual winner, I could have had three guesses and still had to leave the money lying on the table. The winning strategy had been sitting under my nose my entire career, but I had failed to see it.

As a matter of fact, now that I have wandered this personal journey, I am shocked at the overwhelming lack of understanding in the entire financial industry about how money works, how it is best accumulated for the long haul, and what financial tools serve as the best conduit for long-term accumulation.

As a general rule, insurance agents don't understand it (I didn't for most of my career), financial planners don't understand it, the financial media doesn't understand it, and certainly stock brokers don't understand it. A large majority of all individuals working in the financial industry are working half-blind. They are spewing facts and figures that are half true (and maybe totally false) because they are only listening to the supposed experts in their own field. They have no understanding of the entire financial landscape, and in their minds, as long as they continue making a good personal income, why should they care?

I was determined to move beyond that level of understanding. Even if I didn't like what I discovered. Even if all of my former beliefs about money and accumulation proved incorrect. I was going to make an honest and fair search.

I did. And the journey was exhilarating.

It is my fervent hope that the knowledge I gained from my personal journey proves to be the most profitable financial information you have ever received. I hope this book makes a lasting impact in your life, the life of your family, and the future of the community in which you live.

If you follow the masses, you will end up like the masses. If you dare to be different, your life will have a significant impact. Live well. Oh, and by the way, don't let greed or fear be your guide ... they will always steer you wrong.

2

Why is Everybody in Such a Financial Mess?

Have I gotten your attention? I hope so, because your financial future depends on it. But before we dive in and explore why the government is the only eventual winner for those who fund a tax-qualified retirement plan, I need to lay some additional ground work. You know the saying, "You can lead a horse to water, but you can't make him drink." Well, the same is true of humans in the financial realm.

I could lay before you a plan that makes all the sense in the world. I could show you how to avoid tax on your savings. I could razzle-dazzle you with all sorts of new information. But as good as those things are, you must know that your financial success will not be accomplished by your *knowledge* of those things. Your financial success depends solely on *your actions*.

In my fifteen years in this business, I have discovered nine amazingly common problems that we all face. I have seen them in such unanimity that I am coining a new phrase and calling them *Financial Landmines*. Truly, I have never met anyone, and I mean *anyone*, who hasn't struggled with some, most, or all of these problems.

So, if these *Financial Landmines* are common to us all, and they hinder us from making good financial choices, then we must address each of them before I give you my solution or it would be no better than leading a horse to water who wasn't thirsty.

I want the next section of this book to make you thirsty. Thirsty to make wise choices. Thirsty to do things differently. Thirsty to turn over a new leaf in managing your finances. And thirsty to create a plan that works for your personal situation and then stick to it for the long-term.

Please understand that this is a critical part of the book for everyone, even for those of you who are managing your money successfully. Trust me, there will come a day that one of these landmines will knock on your door so loudly or appear so lovely that you won't be able to deny its call. I want more for you than that. I promise that if you will avoid these common *Financial Landmines* you will find investment success that few have experienced.

Then, and only then, will you be fully prepared to take advantage of the new insights that this book has to offer.

And if you avoid both the nine *Financial Landmines and* implement the *Tax-Free Retirement* strategy that I lay out, then you will find yourself in a position to revolutionize not only your financial future, but quite literally the future of your family, your community, and very possibly the world.

Though those comments seem like quintessential overstatements, you will see how true they are once you conclude the last chapter of the book.

Okay! Are you ready? Let's jump into those *Financial Landmines* ....

Part II: Avoiding the 9 Financial Landmines

3

Landmine #1 – Lack of Planning

How is it that hundreds of thousands of Americans each year find themselves at retirement age without the necessary funds to be able to retire? What happened? Who's at fault? Is the government to blame?

Many people go to school, get a job, work forty years, retire temporarily, but find they can't afford to live; so at age sixty-five or older, they go back to work at McDonalds and die during the lunch rush with a spatula in one hand and a sesame seed bun in the other. Okay, maybe it happens a little differently than that, but without the proper planning, you too may find yourself setting a new Guinness World Record as the oldest person ever to assemble the "two all-beef patties, special sauce, lettuce, cheese, pickles, onions, on a sesame seed bun." (Ray Kroc is smiling in his grave that I just wrote that quote by memory, nearly thirty years after his ad campaign.) Few people ever stop long enough during the hustle and bustle of everyday life to ask some important questions: *How much money will I need to retire? At what age do I want to retire? And how will the money get there?*

Don't make that mistake.

It's easy to throw around numbers like a million dollars, but most people have no idea how much they would need to save every month to build a bank account consisting of one million dollars. Let me ask you right now, at 8% interest, how much would you have to save starting today to have one million dollars at age 65? What if the interest rate were 6% or 12%? You don't know? Why not? You see, the number one obstacle to effective saving is exactly this: People don't have a plan.

I'll be willing to bet that there isn't 1 out of 10,000 people that could answer that question without sitting down with a financial calculator to figure it out. Our society trains us *not* to know. As a matter of fact, it trains us not to care. We are called to spend, spend, spend, and once the money is gone, to pull out the plastic and spend some more.

Most people give their attention and effort to how much they are going to spend, not to how much they are going to save. Or if they do save, their only plan is to sock away whatever is left over after all the bills are paid. The problem? There is never anything left over – regardless of whether the person is making $20,000 or $200,000. Without a plan, it *all* gets spent.

Saving money has almost become un-American, un-patriotic. In their best-selling book, *Your Money or Your Life*, Joe Dominguez and Vicki Rubin report that, "The savings rate (savings as a percent of disposable income) was 4.5 percent in 1990 (and was as low as 4.1 percent in 1988), whereas in 1973 Americans saved an average of 8.6 percent. The Japanese, by the way, save over 15 percent of their disposable income."[1]

What's wrong with this picture? Most Americans don't have a plan. Remember, *people don't plan to fail, they fail to plan.* As I look at the above statistics, it is evident to me that we are a nation of individuals who have lost the art of saving. We see a toy and we buy it. We drive by a bigger house and we get it. We envy our neighbor's car, so we duplicate (or surpass) it.

Maybe you find yourself losing the savings battle because you don't have a plan. What can you do? The answer is easy – build one. Let me walk you through the practical steps necessary to build and *implement* (this is the key) a practical and workable plan.

Step 1: Set a Goal

Decide how much money you need (or want) to accumulate and how many years you have to reach that goal. For instance, if you are currently 35 years old and want to build a nest egg of $1,500,000 by the time you reach 65 (which by the way would only be worth $610,540 in today's dollars with a modest 3% inflation), how much would you need to save each month? I think you'll be shocked at the result.

Monthly contribution necessary for a 35 year old to save $1,500,000 by age 65

Interest Rate Monthly	Contribution Necessary
4%	$2,161
6%	$1,493
8%	$1,006
10%	$664
12%	$429

(This table does not take into consideration the *reduction* in savings due to taxes paid on the interest during the accumulation years.)

The only variable in this chart is the interest rate. The length of time for each example is exactly the same. I told you the results would be shocking. I've heard it said that compound interest is the eighth wonder of the world – now you see why.

PATRICK KELLY

As a little child, I remember my mother asking me an interesting question. Maybe you've been asked the same one. She was using this question as a teaching tool. It was obviously a good one, because it has stayed with me through all my years.

"Patrick," she said, "would you rather have someone give you $1,000,000 or a penny that doubled its value every day for a month?"

"A million dollars for sure!" I replied. That was when a million dollars was all the money in the world. I was sure it would take a thousand years of doubling for that penny to be worth a whole million dollars.

She looked at me with a smile and said, "I want you to go and figure out how much that penny would be worth after a month of doubling every day and then come back and tell me which one you would rather have."

"Okay." I said, and I was off to begin my manual calculations.

It's a good exercise to work though manually to see when that penny really begins to grow in value, but I'll save you the steps and amaze you with the answer. That penny is worth almost *eleven times* that million dollar offer for a 30-day month ($10,737,418.24 to be exact), and *twenty-one and a half times* more than the million-dollar offer for a 31-day month ($21,474,836.48 to be exact.) Now which would you rather have?

Are you beginning to see the incredible power of compound. interest?

Step 2: Pay Yourself First

Now that you have the makings for an effective roadmap for your future investment goals, how are you actually going to find the money in your budget to put away for the future? If you're like most people, you realize that most of the time there is more month than money.

So if you are maxed out right now, you may be wondering where the money is going to come from to fulfill your newly designed plan? The answer is a very simple principle that any financial planner worth his or her salt would espouse, yet a plan that very few people actually practice. It is this: Pay yourself first.

Who is the first person to take any money from your monthly income? Uncle Sam, of course. He never misses. No matter how much or how little you make, he always gets his cut. Why? He gets paid first. There is always money for him to take. How well would it work if Uncle Sam said, "Go ahead and pay all of your bills and obligations, buy all of your concert tickets and fund all of your vacations. Then at the end of the month, send us whatever you have left over." One thing's for sure. We'd have a lot fewer bureaucrats!

Whatever the government might be, they aren't dumb. They know full well that if they waited to get their cut until after you paid your bills, their work would be in desperate straits. There would be nothing left over, just like there is nothing left over for you right now. And what do you do to compensate for this reduction in your income, compliments of Uncle Sam? You adjust your living standards to fit within the amount that is left over (hopefully.)

What would happen if the next time you received your check you said, "You know, I can't afford to pay taxes anymore. I need that money for next month's trip to Hawaii." It wouldn't be long before you found yourself living with a new friend named Bubba, in a ten-by-ten cement room with steel windows, with no more worries about paying taxes (or monthly bills for that matter.)

People pay taxes, and they pay them out of the *first dollars* they earn.

Why do you treat Uncle Sam better than you treat yourself? Intentionally, you don't; it's just that you don't think of it in those terms. The key to investment success is to do for yourself what the government so kindly does for you. Set aside a percentage of your income, and *save it right off the top.* I would recommend you save *at least ten percent of your gross income* right off the top. And the best way to do that is to treat the amount just like your taxes or any other bill. Pay it first, and automatic deduction is best.

Ten percent may seem like an impossible amount, but it isn't. You may be surprised to find that you don't even miss it. At least that much money filters through most people's fingers each month on such things as lattes, fast food, and trinkets they don't need. Why? Simply because the money is there, begging to be spent. If you take it away first, and create a false sense of scarcity, I don't believe you will lessen your standard of living one bit, you will just reduce the number of goodies you need to sell at your next garage sale.

When you are tempted to spend from your new savings account, or to fudge just a little this month – don't! Pretend your investment money is just as impossible to reach as the taxes you pay each and every month. If things are truly tight, plan your budget around this newly reduced amount. It may mean that you have to reevaluate your budget and cut something out that is not a necessity, but it is my experience that you will hardly notice the difference.

This has always been my motto: It's a lot easier to spend money that you've over-saved than it is to save money that you've over-spent.

Step 3: Start Today and Be Consistent

The last step is very simple – start today and don't waver from your plan. I'm going to address this in more detail in the following chapter.

Just to recap, these are the three simple steps of building and implementing a workable plan:

Step 1: Set a goal.

Step 2: Pay yourself first.

Step 3: Start today and be consistent.

4

Landmine #2 – Procrastination

In the last section you saw by our investment table how dramatic an effect the percent of return can have on the future outcome of your investment. In this section we will look at the other significant factor in determining the size of your future nest egg – time.

"In 1626, Native Americans sold what is now called Manhattan Island, New York, to white settlers for a pile of trinkets worth only $24. Manhattan's value as real estate is now appraised at $23.4 billion. But if the Native Americans had sold those trinkets for $24 cash and placed the money in a 6% compound-interest account, their investment would now total $27,600,000,000. And if today's Native Americans had inherited this fortune, they could buy back Manhattan and still have over $4 billion left in their account!

That isn't to say the Native Americans got a fair deal, but rather to illustrate that what seems like a little bit might be a lot more than you thought. In other words, great accomplishments don't necessarily require a huge initial investment, the talent of a genius, an incredible windfall, or a superhuman effort. Great accomplishments are possible for anyone who can muster just a little bit and then keep at it with persistence."[2]

Let me illustrate the power that time has on your investment one other way. If, on the day Benjamin Franklin was born in 1706, his parents had deposited one cent in an account earning 8%, Mr. Franklin's heirs would now have a windfall of over $53 million (although after nine generations or so, that's quite a few people to split it with.)

The point is clear – *time has a huge effect on your investment.* Twenty-four dollars becomes $27.6 billion and $.01 turns into over $53 million. Of course these are time periods that are much longer than your personal life expectancy, but it is important to know that you can harness this same power and put it to work for you during *your* lifetime.

Let me tell you one last story. It's a story about two individuals named Jill and Mark. At age 19, Jill started investing $2,000 a year with a compound interest rate of 10%. After only *eight years* (age 26) she stopped investing and left her $16,000 to grow until age 65.

Mark, on the other hand, because of life's demands, waited until he was 27 (the year Jill stopped) to begin saving for his retirement. He was still young and he was proud of his early start and his attention to his financial well-being. He also contributed $2,000 per year to his retirement, but he contributed for *39 years*, each year from age 27 until the year he retired at age 65. His contribution over those 39 years had been $78,000. (He started only eight years after Jill, but contributed $62,000 more dollars.)

The big question is this: "Who has more money at retirement?" If you said Jill, you're right. The value of her investment at age 65 is $1,035,160, while Mark's is worth only $883,185. See the chart below.

	Jill		Mark	
Age	Contribution	Year-end Value	Contribution	Year-end Value
19	$2,000	$2,200	-0-	-0-
20	2,000	4,620	-0-	-0-
21	2,000	7,282	-0-	-0-
22	2,000	10,210	-0-	-0-
23	2,000	13,431	-0-	-0-
24	2,000	16,974	-0-	-0-
25	2,000	20,872	-0-	-0-
26	2,000	25,159	-0-	-0-
27	-0-	27,675	$2,000	$2,200
28	-0-	30,442	2,000	4,620
29	-0-	33,487	2,000	7,282
30	-0-	36,835	2,000	10,210
31	-0-	40,519	2,000	13,431
32	-0-	44,571	2,000	16,974
33	-0-	49,028	2,000	20,872
34	-0-	53,930	2,000	25,159
35	-0-	59,323	2,000	29,875
36	-0-	65,256	2,000	35,062
37	-0-	71,781	2,000	40,769
38	-0-	78,960	2,000	47,045
39	-0-	86,856	2,000	53,950
40	-0-	95,541	2,000	61,545
41	-0-	105,095	2,000	69,899
42	-0-	115,605	2,000	79,089
43	-0-	127,165	2,000	89,198
44	-0-	139,882	2,000	100,318
45	-0-	153,870	2,000	112,550
46	-0-	169,257	2,000	126,005
47	-0-	186,183	2,000	140,805

48	-0-	204,801	2,000	157,086
49	-0-	225,281	2,000	174,995
50	-0-	247,809	2,000	194,694
51	-0-	272,590	2,000	216,364
52	-0-	299,849	2,000	240,200
53	-0-	329,834	2,000	266,420
54	-0-	362,834	2,000	295,262
55	-0-	399,099	2,000	326,988
56	-0-	439,009	2,000	361,887
57	-0-	482,918	2,000	400,276
58	-0-	531,201	2,000	442,503
59	-0-	584,321	2,000	488,953
60	-0-	642,753	2,000	540,049
61	-0-	707,028	2,000	596,254
62	-0-	777,731	2,000	658,079
63	-0-	855,504	2,000	726,079
64	-0-	941,054	2,000	800,896
65	**-0-**	**1,035,160**	**2,000**	**883,185**

You may be scratching your head and saying, "Wait a minute, how can that be?" The answer is simple – *the amazing power of time* in the compound-interest equation. It truly is astounding, isn't it?

After that last example, you may be thinking "Oh great, I'm 43 years old, and I haven't done anything to save for my future. It's all over. There's no hope."

Don't get discouraged. It's never too late to begin. If you take advantage of the principles of this book and put yourself in a position to harvest tax-free dollars in retirement, you can supercharge your retirement years by avoiding tens of thousands – if not hundreds of thousands – of dollars of tax that can now be assimilated into *your* budget instead of going to line the eternally voracious bureaucratic coffers.

Let me ask you another question. If you wanted a nice, big oak tree in your front yard, when would have been the best time to plant it? Certainly a hundred years ago or more, right? However, if that tree was never planted, when would be the next best time to plant it? You got it – today!

This same principle holds true in the world of investing. When would have been the best time to start investing? The day you were born. But unless you were an exceptionally gifted infant, it probably didn't happen (unless of course a parent or grandparent was wise enough to know this principle.) So, just like the oak tree, if you haven't started, the best time to begin is right now – today.

If it makes so much sense to start early, why do people wait? Because life is geared that way. When you're in your twenties, thirties, and even forties, life throws you demand after demand, all of them urgent. It's a time when people are trying to get established and find their path. They start their career, get married, add children to their family, buy their first house, put new tires on their ten-year-old Chevy, put braces on junior No. 2, buy a car for junior No. 1, and a hundred-and-one other things that distract them from beginning to save for their future. Their need for money is right now. Life is expensive and saving becomes only a dream. Therefore, many people put off investing until that mythical "someday" when they have more money. Yet in most cases that "someday" never comes. Life's demands have a way of increasing faster than one's income. There is only one way to break the cycle. We addressed it in step 2 in the last chapter – pay yourself first!

Maybe now you can see why I am taking the time to walk you carefully through these landmines before I introduce you to the powerful investment vehicle that will allow you to build tax-free wealth. If you don't have this foundation in place, you could easily step on one of these hidden explosives and find yourself financially crippled. Without this foundation, the profits from this new strategy won't mean a thing. You'll spend them, waste them, or assimilate them into your already over-stuffed budget. You'll do anything but actually save them.

Thankfully, unlike tax-qualified retirement plans, you can begin the program I am going to present to you at *any* age. I have started them for each of my four children when each was under a year old. Unlike most (if not all) other tax-advantaged vehicles, this strategy will allow you to harness the principle in this chapter – time – unlike any other vehicle in the investment marketplace today, because there is no age at which you must stop investing or start withdrawing.

As you can hopefully see, this chapter is not just a minor formality for the *Tax-Free Retirement* strategy; it is the very foundation for true financial success. For me to present the *Tax-Free Retirement* program to you without showing you how to tiptoe carefully through the field of hidden *Financial Landmines* would be like sending a battalion of new recruits into battle without a battle plan. They would be doomed to certain death, and so would your finances.

I hope by the time you read these principles, you too will feel as strongly about them as I do. Please don't give in to your temptation to jump ahead without taking the time to plan appropriately – your financial success depends on it.

5

Landmine #3 – Getting on the Wrong Side of Mr. Interest

Let me tell you a story about a man named Mr. Interest.[3] As a matter of fact, you know this individual. He's your employee and he works for you around the clock. While you sleep. While you work. While you're on vacation.

He's the hardest worker who has ever lived, and he works for you. The question is, what have you employed him to do? Have you hired him to work *for* you; or is he spending every second of every day working *against* you?

He can be your slave whose free services profit you richly, or he can be an incessant bill collector whose sole job is to charge you a wage, twenty-four hours a day, seven days a week, 365 days a year.

Which will it be?

In my line of work, I get the opportunity to work with many different business owners. Some are productive, some are not. Some present themselves professionally, some do not. Some have a vision for their future, some do not. But one common denominator I've found in *every* business is this ... employing good quality, faithful workers, who contribute to profit, is essential.

Employing Mr. Interest to work for you is like hiring a person to come to work, make you money, but never accept a paycheck. On the other hand, hiring Mr. Interest to work against you is like paying an employee every day of the year (including weekends and holidays) to run your business into the ground and give all your profits away to the competitor.

You definitely want to be on the right side of Mr. Interest.

Let me put this principle in concrete terms. I know an individual, I'll call him John, whose dream was to have a boat large enough to take out for a week or more at a time. It didn't need to be extravagant, just enough to explore the great waters of the San Juan Islands and into Canada. After years of waiting, the day finally arrived.

John's credit union told him there was no problem qualifying for a loan. He scoured newspapers, boat magazines, and boat dealerships for good deals, and finally, one day he found it. He found the boat he'd been dreaming about for years. And he did what any healthy, red-blooded American would do; he bought it – on credit, of course. The boat's final sticker price with tax and licensing came to about $43,000, modest by all boating standards. John took out a ten year loan, to keep the payments at a minimum, at an interest rate of 7.75%. It was a good deal to be sure, and he knew the memories he would build with his family would be worth every penny. But what John didn't fully understand was that at the very moment he inked the deal, Mr. Interest punched in on the time clock and began his relentless crusade against him.

You see, the memories John would build with his family would be far more costly than $43,000. Far more. Let me illustrate.

John's monthly payment for the boat was around $520 a month. Once he added in moorage, maintenance, fuel, and insurance, his monthly payments averaged out to be around $800 per month. John knew all these figures even before he purchased the boat. They were costs he was happy to pay to fulfill a life-long dream.

However, John hadn't figured in the billing fee of Mr. Interest. When I sat down with John, I ran some numbers with him. Numbers he was shocked to see. I took that $800 per month and figured out how much John was going to pay for this dream boat over the next ten years at 7.75% interest. That figure came to $96,813.82. Okay, so his $43,000 boat was going to cost him a little more than $43,000. The family memories were still worth $100,000 he figured, more in an attempt to pacify his growing angst. However, I pointed out to him that that was only a *fraction* of Mr. Interest's actual bill.

"John, you may pay $96,813 for the boat, but how much would you have accumulated if you had saved that money for your retirement?"

"I have no idea," he said. So, with the assistance of my financial calculator we set off to find the answer.

"What do you feel is a fair average growth rate on your money between now and your retirement?"

"I don't know. Does 12% seem too high? That seems like a number I've heard kicked around before."

I explained to him that 12% was a bit aggressive, but for illustration sake I was happy to proceed with his suggestion.

"Okay, if you put that same $800 into an investment vehicle (whose accumulation does not get taxed) for the next 10 years and you averaged a 12% return, you would amass a savings of $184,030.95."

"Wow!" he said, his eyes the size of small saucers.

"John, how many years do you plan to work?"

"Oh, I'd say another thirty-five years or so."

"Okay. We have already calculated the cost for the first ten years. But if we want to see what that boat is actually costing you, we need to figure out how that amount will compound over the next twenty-five years. We want to know what that boat payment is actually costing you in retirement dollars."

"I'd never thought of it that way."

"Don't feel badly. Most people don't." I said consolingly. "Now, if we take that $184,030.95 and project its growth over the next 25 years at 12%, without adding another penny, we come up with a total cost of $3,641,690.25."

Now not only were his eyes the size of saucers, but the tremor of his lower jaw hitting my desk measured a 6.0 on the Richter scale.

"You've got to be kidding. My forty-three thousand dollars worth of family memories is really costing me over *three and a half million dollars* in retirement income? I love my family, but I had no idea how much this dream was really costing me."

"Yep." I said, letting the numbers speak for themselves.

"I can't get over the fact that a forty-thousand dollar boat is costing me millions of dollars!"

"You now see the importance of being on the right side of Mr. Interest," I said.

"No kidding. If I invested the money that I am now spending on the boat, I could easily pay cash for the boat later and still have a lot left over."

"Now you're getting the idea." I said. But unfortunately, I wasn't finished with John; I had to dig the knife a little deeper. "John, I hate to be the bearer of bad news, but it's even worse than the picture we've already painted."

"What do you mean?" he said.

I wanted to take John down the next path that most people never travel and show him how money that is heavily taxed upon withdrawal will make these numbers even more grim.

"John, right now where are you saving money?"

"Well, I was putting a thousand dollars a month into my 401(k) at work, but I'm reducing that amount to two hundred so I can buy this boat. I decided the dream was worth it. At least I thought it was before this conversation."

"So, if you weren't buying that boat, you would be continuing to fund your 401(k)?" I asked.

"Yes."

"Do you realize that once you start taking money out of that account every penny is taxed as income?"

"Well, sort of. I never really stopped to think about it. All I know is that I get the tax write off today. I like that."

"Sure you do. We all like saving money on our taxes. But you are not really saving money on your taxes; you are only compounding the problem."

"What do you mean?"

"Well, in very simplistic terms, if that three and a half million were in an account that you could access tax-free then how much of *your* money is in that account?"

"I'm sure I'm missing the point because it seems too obvious, but I'd say three and a half million."

"No tricks here. You are tracking well and your answer is correct. You'd have the full three and a half million."

Then I posed the next question to him. "If you accumulate that same amount of money in your 401(k) or other tax-qualified retirement plan, how much of your money is in that account?

"Okay, now I'm really starting to worry, but I'd say the same amount. You just said that I would have that much in the account, so why would it be any different?"

"You're right, partially," I said. "Your account statement would read three and a half million dollars, but is that what *you* would really have?"

"Obviously not, by the way you're asking the question, but I'm not sure I follow."

"Well, who else has a stake in your retirement account?"

"No one. It's just in my name."

I was starting to smile as I said, "That's not entirely true. You see, since every penny in your account needs to be taxed upon withdrawal. The IRS is about a 30% stakeholder in your account. And that's if you live. If you die, the IRS is more like a 35% stakeholder. Actually, since we don't know what tax rates will do in the future, that number could be lower or it could be drastically higher. But let's assume the tax rate to be 30% on the funds while you are living, just to be safe." Now my smile was fully engaged. "Did you know you were saving money for Uncle Sam's retirement?"

Obviously, no one had ever really explained to John what would happen to his tax-qualified retirement plan in the distribution phase, because he sat there without saying a word, slipping into a financial depression before my very eyes. I decided I better finish quickly so I could throw him a life ring before he sunk completely.

"John, I'm telling you this for two reasons. One, most people don't know this, and in the later years they find themselves burdened with excessive taxes they don't need to pay. The good news is that I can show you a better way, so you can begin saving 100% of your retirement account for you and not let Uncle Sam touch one penny.

"The second reason is to show you the power of this other strategy. You see, in order to accumulate three and a half million dollars of *your* money inside your tax-qualified plan you would need to amass a full *five million* dollars. Why? Because Uncle Sam gets his 30% cut. However, if you use a different strategy, then you can keep the full account value and realize the entire amount for yourself. So, to completely depress you, that fiberglass palace of family memories is actually costing you somewhere between $3,500,000 and $5,000,000, depending on how wise you are with your investment choices."

"Yes, Patrick, you have depressed me, but I think I'll recover pretty quickly," he said with a chuckle of his own as he picked up his phone. "One thing is for sure, you have opened my eyes to some pretty interesting ideas. How come no one else has told me these things?"

Once again, I was faced with the perennial question that only had one answer. "John, as weird as it sounds, the only answer that I can come up with when people ask me that question is because most of the so-called professionals don't really understand it either."

I had hardly finished my last sentence before John was dialing the number of his local yacht broker, asking him to sell his million-dollar dream boat.

For the first time in his life, John fully understood that time was indeed money, for that was what allowed Mr. Interest to work his true magic.

Before I conclude this chapter, I want to clarify a couple of important issues. There is *nothing* wrong with owning a boat. There is nothing wrong with desiring to build lasting memories with your family. And there is actually nothing wrong with buying a big ticket item on credit. It's all up to you. But beware. There *is* something wrong with not fully understanding the power of Mr. Interest.

Money is not the most important thing in life. Far from it. This example was not given to entice you to sell everything you have and hoard money for your future savings. Rather, this story was shared simply to illustrate the incredible power of compound interest and how much it can cost you to be on the wrong side of our friend or foe, Mr. Interest.

6

Landmine #4 – Desire
for Instant Gratification

In our country, waiting is anathema. Think about what has happened to our society over the last twenty years. Take banks for example. Their first move was to add a drive-up window so that their customers wouldn't have to take the time to get out of their car. Obviously that wasn't quite good enough, so cash machines were added for even faster service. But that, too, must have been inconvenient, because soon after that came the advent of the drive-through-cash-machine. However, that wasn't the end of the line either, because now banks offer the ultimate efficiency in banking and allow you to make all your transactions on the telephone or via the Internet, any time of day, any day of the week.

But banks are just one example. Think about the other revolutions we have made in the art of instant gratification. A leisurely sit-down meal has become a grease bomb at a drive-through burger joint. Someone with seven items in the express lane at the grocery store has almost become justification for a lawsuit. And going shopping requires nothing more than a browse through a catalog or a channel on television.

We as Americans loathe anything that causes us to slow down our frantic pursuit. We hate lines. We hate traffic jams. And we hate paying cash.

Cash represents spending money we actually possess. And the concept of spending only the money that we earn is branded as prehistoric thinking. We have home loans and car loans and business loans and boat loans and credit card loans. And then when our loan ratio is about ready to burst at the seams, we take out loans to pay our loans. We use our Master Card® to pay our Visa®. If we can't afford it, we charge it. The thought of paying cash is a thing of the past – but it doesn't have to be.

I heard on the radio that credit card companies send out *two and a half billion* applications every year – that's an average of twenty-five applications for every man, woman, and child in America; and that was probably five years ago. I can only imagine what that number is today. When you consider that many of the people in our country never receive a single one of these applications, that means that some people (like you and me) receive over one hundred of these irritating applications every year.** The financial world has not only made it possible for Americans to crank up their debt, they expect it. How can someone with a lust for more turn down the offer for "free" money one hundred times a year? The answer is simple. They can't.

Right after I heard this statistic, I performed a small experiment. Instead of throwing away all the credit card offers I received in the mail, I decided to keep them and see just how much credit I could accumulate if I wanted to. I was going to do this for an entire year, but I couldn't. I had to quit. The sheer volume was utterly ridiculous; I had to dedicate an entire file drawer to hold all of these credit card offers. I averaged about four offers per week, each one offering $10,000 or more. (This doesn't even count the multiple offers I received each month for $100,000 to take out a home equity loan.)

If you put a calculator to those numbers, which are conservative at best, you come up with substantially more than two million dollars of credit card offers. Can you believe it? I don't know how many of those a person could get issued, but it is safe to say that the average American could secure tens and very likely hundreds of thousands of dollars in credit card potential in a period of twelve short months. If that isn't a temptation for someone lacking moral integrity, I don't know what is. This person could throw the party of the century, live high on the hog for years, travel the world, buy all sorts of expensive toys, and just when the clock was about to strike midnight and Cinderella's coach was ready to turn back into a pumpkin, this person could shell out a measly $500 to their local attorney, file bankruptcy, and wipe the slate clean. No criminal charges. No ramifications. Just a slap on the hand and a bad credit rating for seven years. If you think I'm making this up, think again. People are doing this every day, to varying degrees, without a single tinge of guilt or responsibility.

Is it any wonder that people are in financial trouble? Most folks are way over their head in unsecured, consumer debt. And the big question is: Why? No one likes being in debt. No one likes credit card balances. So why do the masses do it? The answer is simple – people don't like to wait. The motto of our time is, "I want it, and I want it now." Waiting to purchase something is for those financial cripples who can't get a credit card.

But what these people don't realize is that they unknowingly have one foot poised over a deadly explosive. The desire for instant gratification is a lethal, financial landmine. And it is not choosy whom it destroys. Its effects can be merely crippling, but more often than not, they're lethal.

So how do you avoid the fate of this deadly foe? *Think before you spend!* And *only* spend what you have in your bank account, *not* what you have in your credit limit.

Does that mean you can't buy a home on credit? No. Does that mean it is wrong to finance a brand new car? No. But, I give you a strong warning against car loans and other consumer debt of any kind. Be careful. This kind of debt is a dangerous landmine we're talking about, not some child's play toy.

Debt is the budget item that eats up most people's savings. It is a financial anchor, chained tightly around their legs. People find themselves not being able to save, because they've become enslaved. Enslaved to the debt that has resulted from their passion to buy things, right now, today. Not only does this lifestyle have a crippling effect on their future savings, but it is also devastating to any chance of maintaining a healthy, financial morale. This person is always the proverbial "day late and dollar short." He's always paying off yesterday's purchases instead of saving for tomorrow's needs.

Be careful of this reverse planning! However, if this message has reached you a little too late and you find you've already accumulated more debt than you can pay off, I encourage you to do something very un-American. Are you ready? Follow these simple instructions:

Step 1: Right now, march into your kitchen or your den and grab a pair of sharp scissors.

Step 2: Proceed to remove all of your credit cards – yes all of them – from your wallet or purse.

Step 3: Next, take those sharp scissors and cut to shreds every one of those little pieces of plastic.

Step 4: After this procedure is complete, stand up and march out of the room chanting at the top of your lungs, "No more debt! No more debt! No more debt!"

Sept 5: Enjoy the unexpected feeling of freedom you now experience.

Okay, maybe steps four and five seem a bit excessive, but I'm totally serious about steps one through three. If you do this, you will help to ensure that you will not put yourself further into debt. It does nothing, however, to remedy the poor spending choices of your past. But don't despair. You will find that once you begin to spend only the money you make, and are not progressively digging yourself deeper and deeper in debt, you will be able to allocate more money each month to pay off your existing loans or to save for your future.

As you work to bring your spending into check – think! Ask yourself if you really need the item you desire or if it is just a fleeting want. It's these fleeting wants that usually end up collecting dust in our garage.

One conservative financial author takes this idea a step further and encourages people to develop a "Want-List" for large ticket items. You get to define large. For some it may be $50, for others it may be $500. This want-list is a very short list, because it can only contain *one* item at a time. And that one item must stay on this list for 90 days before the purchase is made. What usually happens he says, is that sometime during that 90-day period, he finds an item he wants more than the one on the list. So he replaces it. But once he does that, the 90-day clock starts all over again. This has protected him from making many unnecessary and unwanted purchases.[4]

Something different may work for each one of us, but the principles are the same:
- Spend less than you earn.
- Don't buy on impulse.
- Resist your desire for instant gratification.

** Just recently I was made aware of a website, *optoutprescreen.com*. This is a website that allows you remove yourself from receiving pre-qualified credit offers in the mail. It is simple, takes less than a minute to complete, and supposedly has the possibility of raising your credit score.

7

Landmine #5 – Following the Masses

In J.D. Salinger's book, *The Catcher in the Rye*, the main character, Holden Caulfield, has a dream. In this dream he pictures many children running through a tall field of rye. However, unbeknownst to the children, they are running straight toward a deadly cliff that sinisterly waits for them at the far side of the field.

This scene is not unlike the investment climate in our world today. The average person saving for retirement is running through a field of tax-qualified retirement plans without knowledge of what lurks on the other side. They are running carefree, enjoying the beauty of the day, content with life as they know it. But things are about to change. The pleasure of today's tax write-offs will soon materialize as tomorrow's tax nightmares; and the sunny day which they are now enjoying will soon darken with the storm clouds of tomorrow's tax-burdens. Everything is about to change. The cliff is coming. And the masses don't have a clue.

Why shouldn't we follow the masses? I'll make this very simple. *The masses are usually wrong.* Let's look at the history of the stock market for a little example. If you look throughout history, what do the masses do? Just the opposite of what they should. They buy when they should be selling and they sell when they should be buying. The masses act on instinct, but most financial markets don't. They require a reverse kind of instinct. One that runs contrary to our inborn nature.

And who are the masses? You know them well. It's you and I, your neighbor next door, your co-worker in the next cubicle, the person in your golf foursome or your carpool. If you look at the history of the stock market, by nature, we all do it wrong. And we do it wrong because of two basic human instincts – fear and greed. These two instincts are also helped along by the innate desire for us to be like everyone else. We want to be liked. We don't want to stand out. The bottom line is, we want to be like everyone else. It's a cycle we must break if we want to achieve the great things that are possible.

Most people saving for retirement need to revisit their kindergarten classes and hear their teachers remind them that just because little Johnny stuck a piece of macaroni up his nose, doesn't mean that you should stick one up your nose as well.

There are certainly times when it is better *not* to follow the lead of others. Kindergarten was one; investing in government-sponsored, tax-qualified plans is another.

In this book, *Tax-Free Retirement,* I want you to know that you no longer need to blindly follow the masses, simply because it is the only path through the field of rye. I want everyone to know that there *does* exist an investment alternative that far exceeds the benefits of today's tax-qualified retirement plans. The secret has been kept too long. Someone owes an apology to you and the rest of the American people for robbing you of the knowledge that has been utilized by the privileged few for decades.

Before you continue to run blindly any longer, stop and evaluate your situation. Study the coming chapters in this book and then decide on your own what is best for your financial future. Stop throwing away money along with the masses. You don't want to suffer for their ignorance.

8

Landmine #6 – The Inertia Factor

Let me give you a warning. I have seen this happen numerous times, and it will probably happen again with you as you read this book. You are going to go through what I call the discovery cycle. Near the end of this discovery cycle lays a large temptation. The temptation to *do nothing* – to read this book and then put it down without allowing yourself to change. Though we don't like to admit it, it is often easier for us to do the things we know, than it is to try something new, even if a new way is more profitable.

If my guess is correct, right now you are sensing a new excitement about your financial future. And you should. The information that is yet to come is exciting. However, if you don't overcome the *Inertia Factor,* nothing will change.

I can still remember learning about inertia in my high school physics class. Simply put, it is the energy necessary to get an object in motion. All of us have an inertia point. Think about it. Why do we get out of bed each morning and go to work? We do so because we need to earn money to buy food, obtain shelter, and to enjoy whatever other things our paycheck provides. Therefore we can conclude that the desire to have these things provides enough inertia for us to get up each morning and keep a job, instead of staying home and zoning in front of television re-runs.

Everything you do has an associated inertia factor. Investing is no different. You can read this book and be as charged up as a Virginia firefly, but unless you act on this knowledge, the excitement is purely wasted. It profits you nothing.

But let me assure you, there are many idea junkies out there who get a good buzz off a new idea. They don't have to use it; they just have to learn it. Don't be an idea junkie. Find something that works and focus your energy on that one thing. Instead of trying to put your eggs in different baskets, as we have been told so often to do, it might be better to put them all in one basket and then watch that basket very, very carefully. You see, diversification of our investments is wise, but diversification of our energy is foolish. We can't be a master of all things and expect exceptional returns.

I include this seemingly innocuous landmine in this book because the strategies you are about to learn in the upcoming chapters require action on your part in order to set them into motion. Minor action... but action nonetheless. Very few saving strategies are easier to set up or maintain than the one I am going to introduce you to. As a matter of fact, if it is done correctly, it should take *no* time on your part to manage. Having said that, it does still take the initial effort; effort that could likely save you hundreds of thousands of dollars in taxes in the future.

Resist the temptation to reject what is new or different. Be willing to act when you discover a fantastic opportunity, like the one I'm going to introduce to you in the pages to come. Don't let the *Inertia Factor* force you back to doing the same things you've always done.

I'm sure you've heard the saying, "If you always do what you've always done, you'll always get what you've always got."

It's true.

I hope you will use this book to launch yourself into action to propel yourself down a life-long road of successful savings.

9

Landmine #7 – A Desire to Get Rich Quick

I can only wonder how many fortunes have been lost and families ruined through the greed-driven desire to get rich quickly. This mentality has been elevated to epidemic proportions. Everywhere I turn, I see it's mark on our society – television's infamous infomercials, myriad offers for the latest and greatest multi-level marketing programs, lottery tickets sold weekly by the millions, and the endless offers that appear in my mailbox tempting me with innumerable assurances that I will make my fortune in the next three to six months.

We recently lived through a season in which stock options created a new class of millionaires; individuals who retired in five years or less, having done nothing more than work for the right company at the right time. These instant millionaires caused the rest of society to feel left behind; therefore, many people tried other means to keep up with Mr. "Stock Option" Jones.

Living, for some people, has become nothing more than a sport – the ultimate competition. Many live by the axiom that I've seen paraded above the tailpipe of many cars, "He who dies with the most toys wins."

People buy lottery tickets by the hundreds, they cross their fingers and roll the dice in Vegas, they play the horses at their local track, they follow the stock suggestions of self-professed financial gurus, they buy a stake in Ostrich farms in Oregon and Alpaca ranches in Washington, and they gamble their money away in financial markets they have absolutely no idea how to manage – all to make a fast buck.

Let me assure you of one thing, except for a very small percentage of people, and I mean *very* small (who happen to be both lucky and good), these methods provide only one thing – a sure road to financial ruin.

How can you protect yourself from falling prey to the get-rich-quick tactics that will assault you from every angle? (And you can be certain, there will be times when an offer looks so good that the temptation will be hard to refuse.) Here are two simple principles to follow.

Invest in What You Know

It is tempting to discover a new opportunity and assume that there is an untouched pot of gold just waiting to be taken. And you think to yourself, *who better to do the taking than me?* The problem is, each opportunity has a different set of rules. Far too many people, looking to bypass the natural method of building wealth, set out after this new pot of gold without realizing that they don't have a clue what they're doing. They're throwing money at something that they hope will pay great dividends, like a novice gambler hoping to get lucky enough to draw the right card.

Avoid these get-rich-quick temptations. Invest your money in things you can trust, things that are easy to understand, and things that have been around for decades and which are familiar to you.

And don't trust anyone who tells you they have a "for-sure deal." You may hit it lucky a few times, but eventually you will end up in the poor house.

By the time you are done reading this book, you will find that the tax-free retirement strategy meets this criteria very well. It is a time-tested method that is easy to execute and available to virtually everyone, month after month, year after year.

Remember – The Tortoise Beat the Hare

I said it early in this book, and I'll say it again – slow and steady wins the race. Remember the tortoise in the childhood story, *The Tortoise and the Hare?* Mr. Hare took off like a shot, blowing the tortoise away right from the starting blocks. He was so confident of his abilities that he afforded himself many leisurely stops along the way – distracting himself from his ultimate goal.

In contrast, Mr. Tortoise knew his physical limitations, so to compensate, he just kept at it – hour after hour. He kept plodding toward the goal that awaited him; and sure enough, his persistence paid off. He won the race. He didn't win it because he was the fastest runner but because his personal discipline kept him focused on a goal, and he didn't let himself get distracted by all the temptations along the way. In simplest terms, he just kept at it.

I believe this story holds great significance in the area of personal investing. If you follow the plan in each of these previous chapters, as well as the ones to come, all you need to do now is just keep plugging away at your goal. Don't get sidetracked by some tempting offer that is too good to be true. Almost always, it's exactly that – too good to be true.

Create a simple and achievable plan and then pursue that plan. Let others throw their money to the wind, while yours is diligently working to increase your long-term wealth.

10

Landmine #8 – Lack of Generosity

I remember learning a valuable lesson the year after I graduated from college. I can still recall with clarity the lazy Saturday morning I received the phone call. I probably remember it so well because it was the first one I had ever received since I had embarked on true, post-college bachelorhood. The call was nothing special. It was a cold call, a solicitation. I'm sure I was chosen at random from a phone directory. But I didn't know that at the time.

I don't remember the lady's name, but she was a financial planner at a large company in downtown Seattle. She was calling to see if I would like to come in to her office for a free financial analysis.

I didn't want to waste her time, so I felt the need to give her a clear picture of my meager financial situation. I had just graduated from college and was working as a youth pastor in a local church making a whopping $15,000 per year. I had little money to live on let alone *plan* with.

Now as I look back, it really is a humorous scene. I'm sure she was a new recruit who had quotas to fill. Here I was, earning an income probably below the poverty level, but she didn't miss a beat. No matter how many times I tried to tell her that I really didn't have any money to plan with, she just assured me that it was all the more reason we needed to get together. Finally, for some odd reason, I gave in. I believe the reason I did was because I was naïve to the entire cold call approach. I somehow believed I was one of the privileged few to receive such an offer. Besides, I would get a chance to see Seattle's financial district. I had never been there at that point in my life. In any event, I went.

Our meeting was fairly brief. I filled out a financial question-naire and answered numerous other questions as she scribbled answers on a yellow pad. As the questions wound down, I think she realized that all the creative ideas in the world couldn't make something out of nothing. I didn't have any pressing needs, but I didn't have any money to invest either. She looked at me and said, "I guess you were right. There isn't much I can do for you."

I remember chuckling and feeling a little foolish. Yet I had to remember that it was only because of her insistence that I was there in the first place. But she had a couple of comments for me before I left; and it was in these comments that I gathered a valu-able piece of information.

She said, "Really, you have a very good handle on your financ-es. You have no debt, and are able to budget the money that you make to cover all of your monthly expenses. I also noticed that you give away ten percent of your income to charity. I have found that the people I meet with who give a set portion of their income to charity are also the best savers and money managers."

"That's interesting. Why is that?" I asked.

"Well, I'm not sure, but I think it may be because they have an active plan for their finances. They are aware of what they make and where their money goes. All-in-all they just seem to be the most successful financial managers I meet with."

"Thanks for the input," I said. "If I have a need for your services in the future, I'll give you a call."

We parted with pleasantries, and I was on my way, unaware that the simple conversation that concluded our meeting would stick with me many years later and end up making its way into this book.

I believe she was right; and during my fifteen years helping clients with their money decisions this fact has proven itself time and time again. People who are generous with their money and who enjoy giving to others also find that they are usually not lacking themselves. The Bible confirms this principle when it says, *"Remember this: Whoever sows sparingly will also reap sparingly, and whoever sows generously will also reap generously."*[5] Think about it. It's true. If we smile at someone we pass on the street, they usually smile in return. If we give a complement to someone, they usually proffer the same positive response. Likewise, if we shout at someone in anger, they usually shout back. Truly, we do find that we reap what we sow. We get back what we give out.

In a financial sense, this doesn't mean that we are going to get back some specific ratio of dollars for every dollar we give away; but somehow, people who give part of their income to others and live off of only 90% or less, end up usually doing more with that 90% than other folks do with their 100%. They use the rest of their money more wisely, and usually see more clearly the value of saving for the future.

Many people have short-circuited their finances by trying to hoard all their money. Their shortsightedness has cost them dearly.

If you are one of these individuals, I encourage you to take a step back from your present circumstances and re-evaluate the joy of being able to give part of your income away to your church or to those who are in need – kids without homes, adults without meals, people without hope.

Not only will you manage your finances better if you give part of your income away, but I guarantee you will also find that you receive some rewards that money can't buy – a sense of true satisfaction, a deep joy that lingers long, and a contentment that stays with you well after the money is forgotten.

For the benefit of others, as well as for your own financial well-being, I encourage you to begin to give. If you're married, sit down with your spouse over a cup of coffee and decide where you would like to give part of your income. If you have children, and they are of an appropriate age, include them in these discussions and decisions. What better way is there to pass on a generous spirit to your children than to have them be an active part of the family giving process?

While you're discussing these topics, it is also a great time for you to set some plans for your own savings goals and contributions. To reiterate this point, the better you are at giving away part of your resources, the better you will be at saving part of your resources. That is a true win-win situation!

11

Landmine #9 – Acting like the Future Will Never Arrive

This landmine is unique. It is really the place where the previous eight chapters come together in commonality. It is the glue that makes them stick.

Do you remember as a kid what it felt like to anticipate the arrival of Christmas day? The Thanksgiving feast was no sooner cleared off the table before you began to wonder, "When is Santa going to arrive?" That month between Thanksgiving and Christmas seemed like forever to your childhood perspective. But it always came. And once it arrived, you were sure it was only yesterday that you had been eating a holiday turkey and watching the Thanksgiving Day parade on your mother's lap. The perspective looking forward always seems longer than the perspective looking back.

And so it will be in retirement.

All those years of work. All your anticipation. All those days where retirement seemed to be only an event in someone else's dreams. But before you know it, your time will be here. And once it is you'll look back and say, "Wow, where did all the time go?"

We are not too different from children. We look at the future and act as if it will never come. Intellectually we believe it will, but only *action* speaks our true belief. And according to all of the recent studies I've read, the average American's actions toward saving for retirement are anemic at best.

During the 19th century there lived a dynamic tightrope-walker and showman named Charles Blondin. He was undoubtedly the greatest funambulist that ever lived. His thirst for new and daring stunts was unquenchable. In 1859, at the age of 35, he became the first person to cross Niagara Falls on a tight-rope, 1100 feet long and 160 feet above the water. But just crossing this rope was not enough; history reports that Blondin accomplished this feat numerous times, always with different theatric variations: blindfolded, in a sack, on stilts, carrying a man on his back, and sitting down midway while he cooked and ate an omelette.

Back and forth he went, dazzling the onlookers with his brilliant skill. They were amazed. He made every crossing without a hitch. One day, as the crowd gathered, he stepped off the wire, grabbed an empty wheelbarrow, and stepped back onto the perilous wire. Again, he proceeded to amaze the crowd as he pushed this wheelbarrow back and forth high above the crashing falls.

After he made his way back to the crowd, he stepped off the tight-rope a second time, looked straight at the astonished crowd, and asked this question. "Who believes I can walk across this wire with a wheelbarrow?" Every hand shot up. They had just witnessed this masterful feat.

While all the hands were still raised, he pointed at a young man in the front row and said, "Please sir, get in the wheelbarrow."

Quickly the hands went down, including the young man's, as he slipped away through the crowd, escaping to safety.

The problem was, the man's belief was only intellectual; otherwise, he would have stepped into Blondin's wheelbarrow.

You see, *true belief requires action.* It is action that gives belief its power. This is true in all areas of life. Yet most people's beliefs never venture out of the safe arena of intellect, an arena that requires no commitment and no action.

I tell you this story because it parallels very closely people's actions toward retirement. Intellectually, they plan to retire. Many even have the year marked on their mental calendar. But somewhere along the line, this intellectual plan fails to turn into action. Every year retirement draws closer, and every year they put off the action of setting money aside because of some immediate need shouting very loudly for them to acquiesce.

We tend to forget the future. We believe it is an eternity away, just like we felt about Christmas as a child. But in the same way, it will be here before we know it. And once it arrives, if we didn't start saving soon enough, our only planning will be to figure out where we want to work until the day the mortician decides to give us our last hairstyle.

Don't fall into the trap of believing you have plenty of time before you need to start acting. Start now. The time will pass more quickly than you think.

* * *

As I conclude this section of the book, I want to address one last, important issue; and I feel this is the most appropriate chapter in which to insert these comments. I want to editorialize briefly on the entire subject of retirement so it doesn't seem I am painting with too broad a brush.

This book appears to be making one huge assumption – that you plan to retire. Yet, for many, this may not be the case. I know many individuals that plan to work until either their health takes them out of the marketplace or they die. Many can't stand the thought of being idle. I, myself, am one of those individuals.

Yet, let me take this opportunity to broaden your perspective of retirement. You see, I *do* plan to stop working simply to earn a living, but I *never* plan to stop working to contribute to society. For many, retirement is seen as the long awaited rest after years of drudgery, a time to play after decades of slavery. That is okay. But it is not big enough for me. I want to spend my life doing what I love right now – not waiting until some future date that offers no guarantees. Retirement will simply allow me to pursue my dreams with greater freedom. It will be a chance to give myself completely to what I love without having to worry about providing an income. Retirement should be a time of liberation, a time to pursue your gifts and passions with a new sense of independence, a time to share your wisdom and availability with those who need it most.

When you hear the word retirement, what picture comes to mind? A gray-haired octogenarian whose body is tired from years of labor, or a youthful-spirited individual with a zest for life, who is just reaching his best years? Who says that retirement needs to take place at sixty-five? If you avoid these nine landmines and pursue the incredible opportunity that is waiting for you in the chapters to come, you may just find that you have the option to retire years before you ever thought possible.

I don't know your personal situation, and I don't know your desires. But I do know that it is wise to position yourself so that when you come to that point in your life, be it ten years or forty, you will have choices. And those choices will be the ones you desire, not ones forced upon you due to lack of planning.

Part III: The Hidden Retirement Traps

12

A Story about Bill

I'd like to tell you a story about Bill. Bill is a fictitious thirty-six year old in upper management with a major corporation. However, it wouldn't matter if Bill was a physician, a small business owner, a lawyer, a farmer, a teacher, or an employee of any company large or small. Though figures would differ, the story would be the same.

Bill's current annual salary is $150,000. This is the only company he's worked for since he graduated from college (with honors I might add) and in the fourteen years he has been with this company, he has worked his way up from the front lines due to his faithful and diligent effort. He arrives early and is often the last to leave. He's a company man that everyone respects, and he's sought out for advice from both those who report to him as well as his superiors.

Bill has been married to Marcy for 9 years. Together they have three young children – Lori 6, Billy 4, and Scott 1. He loves his kids and though he doesn't get as much time with them as he would like, he wants what's best for them and is willing to help them in any way, including financially. He hopes that each of them will study hard, go to college (a cost he is planning on paying, just as his father had for him), and find a solid job with a great company, just as he was fortunate to find. Secretly, Bill hopes that one or all of his kids will follow in his footsteps and become future employees of his current company.

Bill's company has a wonderful 401(k) program that he has contributed to faithfully since the beginning of his employment. When he first started with the company he heard a presentation by a financial professional who told him the best place to invest his money was in his company's sponsored 401(k) for three reasons.

First, the presenter said that the company would match up to $1500 per year. This was free money. All he had to do was contribute. That sounded good to Bill. He'd take all the free money he could get.

The second reason he was told this was the best place to save money for his future was that all the income he contributed was tax deferred. At 22, Bill didn't know what that really meant, but the individual went on to explain that all the money he contributed would avoid tax in the year it was put into the plan. So if he made an annual income of $30,000 and contributed $1,500 to the 401(k) he would only be taxed on $28,500. And no tax was owed on the money until he took it out at retirement. The more he contributed the more tax he saved.

The third reason the presenter gave him as to why this was such a great investment method was that when he began withdrawing the money in retirement he would be in a lower tax bracket. Since he would be in a lower tax bracket, he would pay less tax. Again, another exciting prospect in Bill's mind.

Bill has always been good at seeking advice from other professionals so he went to see his CPA as well as one of the top executives of his company.

His CPA told him that investing in his company's 401(k) was a wonderful idea and that it would indeed lower his tax bill each year. The CPA encouraged him to save as much as he could in his 401(k), even while his income was small.

The executive Bill visited (who had been a long time family friend) gave him similar advice. He told Bill that the 401(k) had been the single best investment choice he had ever made. As a matter of fact, it had been the only investment that had really made him money. The executive laughed out loud as he recalled some other investments he had made on "tips" from others – across the board all had been losers.

Bill was really excited to begin his investing career. He had done his homework, he had sought advice, he could avoid taxes now and he didn't have to pay a penny in tax until he began to withdraw money from his account at a *lower* tax rate. What could be better than that?

After these two visits, Bill made a commitment to contribute as much as he could afford to his 401(k), even if it meant he would have to stretch in other areas. During his fourteen years with the company, Bill had been a diligent saver and had accumulated $145,000 in his account. Since his income was meager in the early years, and the demands of his young family were growing, Bill was not able to contribute as much as he had wanted, but he is now proud of his growing nest egg. Now that his current income is much more significant, Bill is able to contribute the full maximum his retirement account will allow. At this rate, and with this continued funding, his benefit statement shows a projected value of $2,669,414 at the age of 62, which is the year Bill hopes to retire. Since he is contributing so much to his 401(k), he is not able to save any additional money, including money toward his children's college education. This concerns Bill, but he figures that with his current income he and Marcy can cut back on some of their extra living expenses when the kids hit college and just pay for each year as the tuition comes due. Bill is 36 and he feels good about his financial future … a financial future that will come to greet him all too quickly.

Let's take a peek at his future, at least in some possible ways it might play out for this shrewd, hard-working individual.

Time has passed quickly. Bill is now 50 and his oldest daughter Lori is a junior in college. It has been a great two years seeing his daughter flourish in a small private university. He has contributed the maximum allowed to his 401(k) every year for the last eleven years. Bill is proud of his wise savings because his 401(k) now sits at $848,819 … he is almost a millionaire.

However, the finances have been far tighter than Bill had expected. Though his income has blossomed to a whopping $259,751, a 4% increase per year, school costs have escalated far more quickly – a rate near 7%. That means that what was once a $30,000 price tag for a year of private tuition now demands a whopping $77,356. He never imagined that one child's college tuition could demand almost 30% of his gross income and almost 40% of his net income. Bill and Marcy have been scrambling for the last two years to try and pay for Lori's tuition out of pocket, but it just wasn't happening. Bill and Marcy have managed to live right up to their increasing income. They have been able to make some cuts, but not enough to pay the entire bill, or even half of it for that matter. Bill doesn't want to tell Lori that she can't attend the college of her dreams, so he knows he'll figure out a way to make it happen.

They have tried looking into financial aid, but with Bill's healthy income they don't qualify. *How can anyone afford to send their kids to college?* Bill wonders.

After they had been rejected by the financial aid office, Bill decided to call the benefits department at his company to inquire about taking money out of his 401(k). Bill was told that he could not make an early withdrawal (before 59 ½) without paying tax on the money as ordinary income. Currently Bill's federal rate has risen to 40%, his state income tax rate has risen to 10%, and on top of that he has a 10% tax penalty for early withdrawal. That means he would have to take out $193,390 from his 401(k) just to be able to pay a $77,356 tuition bill. Ludicrous! That was 22.8% of his *entire* 401(k) for just one year of Lori's tuition. Bill and Marcy have spent the last two years significantly cutting back on all the luxuries they have come to enjoy. But they believe their mission is worth the cost. Besides, it is only for a short season. They have stopped going out to fancy dinners; they canceled plans for nice family vacations for the next few years; they were advised to take out a second mortgage on their home at a rate of 11%; and Bill even came to the conclusion that he would no longer be able to fund his 401(k), at least until the kids were done with college and all their debts were paid off, a decision he really dislikes.

Bill wonders to himself how he could almost be a millionaire on paper but feel flat broke. He has no access to his money without severe penalties. He feels like his own money is being held hostage by the tax system. But he has not worked so hard to sock money away for his retirement only to find 60% of it gobbled up in taxes. A little thought passes through Bill's mind and he wonders for the first time if his 401(k) really had been the best place to save money.

But Bill's financial concerns don't end here. This is also the year that Billy is going to be a freshman in college as well. If one child has been a struggle, how in the world is he going to afford two kids in college? And still a third is not far behind. Bill sees only three options: 1. Tell the kids they need to get a job to help pay for their own tuition. 2. Tell the kids they need to go to less expensive schools. 3. Borrow more money. After talking with Marcy, Bill and Marcy choose number three.

At age 50, Bill is no longer feeling so good about his financial future.

Bill is now 65. The financial storm of his kids' tuition is now a distant memory of years gone by. He and Marcy have survived and are glad they gave their kids the gift of a good education. Yes, he did have to delay his retirement to age 65, but that, too, was a small price to pay. Each of their three children has graduated from college and all three have good jobs. Lori owns her own business and is able to juggle all the demands of a working mother of three. Billy has become an attorney at a local practice in town. And Scott is a high school math teacher in a neighboring community. Bill and Marcy had borrowed what they needed to make it work, and have spent most of the years since then paying off the debt they had accumulated. They were also committed to having their house paid off by the time Bill retired, so they could save that expense in retirement. It is a goal they have achieved just in time. They are now debt free and ready to take on the new adventure of retirement, grandkids, and leisure.

Though Bill had not been able to continue to save money in his 401(k) after Lori's junior year, his original contributions have grown to quite a large sum. His account now stands at a whopping $3,091,808. Bill sits back in his chair and lets out an audible sigh. *Wow, even with those tough years I have still accumulated over three million dollars.* Bill is glad he had chosen to invest in his 401(k). *Good thing I invested as much as I could in those early years. I guess I did receive good advice.*

BUT ... that was before Bill began taking money *out* of his account.

Two months before Bill's retirement a new president of the United States had been elected. Along with a new president, the country had also elected a new Congress and Senate. All three had the same agenda – begin to pay down the horrific debt. The country was serious about attacking the problem and had elected a government it believed would save it from the devastating nightmare of insurmountable debt. The future of America was at stake.

What Americans didn't realize, and what was never spoken during the months of campaigning, was *how* this administration was going to accomplish this task. Those running for office had talked about cutting programs and eliminating governmental waste; the country bought it hook, line, and sinker. No true American wanted to see his or her country go under and many believed it was now or never to salvage the mess. However, along with those original campaign promises lurked the real method of accomplishing the task, which was to raise taxes.

Though taxes had continued to go up over the last 15 years, this was the granddaddy of them all. Bill's federal tax rate has now risen to 55% overnight. He is stunned. To make matters worse, he no longer has any deductions to offset his retirement income. His kids are grown and his house is paid off. All the deductions that he used when he was younger have now evaporated. Every dollar he takes out of his 401(k) is going to be taxed – and taxed hard.

Wait a minute! Bill thinks. *What happened to lower tax rates in retirement because my income is lower? What happened to the idea of saving the tax during the contribution phase because it is better in the long run?*

Bill quickly realizes that the few thousand dollars he had postponed in tax when he was young will now likely cost him well over a million dollars. For the first time it dawns on him that he had never really *avoided* taxes to begin with; he had simply *delayed* them. And by delaying them Bill has only compounded them, making them far, far worse then he could have ever imagined. Worse than anyone could have imagined.

At age 65, Bill is feeling a little sick to his stomach. Uncle Sam is going to ruin his golden years.

It is now five years since Bill's death. He passed away at the age of 80 and Marcy survived her husband by four additional years. It has been nearly a year since she went to rest beside her husband. All three kids appreciated the financial sacrifices of their parents. For over a year they have worked hard at settling all the estate issues. It has been extremely complicated and far more time consuming than any of the three had ever imagined.

But, the biggest shock came when they got the final distribution from their parents 401(k).

In Bill's later years he had confided to his kids about how much money he had saved. He had preserved his original savings of $3,091,808 because he didn't know how long Marcy or he might live and he didn't want to run out of money while one of them was still living. He knew that if he began to spend down his account he might end up with nothing left to sustain Marcy in her later years if he predeceased her, which was a likely event. He didn't want to take that risk. To do this, they lived frugally. With the new tax rates, Bill and Marcy could only live a shadow of the life they were used to. *This* part of his retirement he never shared with his kids.

Once Bill and Marcy's estate was settled and the 401(k) funds were distributed, the kids thought there must certainly be some mistake. Of the nearly three million in their father's account, only $476,368, or 15% was passed onto them. Instead of each child receiving close to $1,000,000, after taxes the three children ended up with just over $150,000 each. Though Scott is nearly retired from teaching math, he knows his skills aren't that rusty. Something has to be in error. He calls a local accountant to show him the situation and after careful review, the CPA tells him that, indeed, the numbers are correct. With the newly instated federal, state, and estate tax rates imposed by congress, taxes have taken a full 85% of his father's qualified retirement account.

The kids are shocked. Why hadn't someone warned their father about this situation? Why hadn't someone warned *them* about this situation? Why hadn't someone showed their father a better way to save for his future?

As they asked around to other financial professionals in the community they quickly realized the answer ... no one they talked to knew of a better way.

Though Bill has long since passed, had he realized what Uncle Sam was going to take from his savings once he and Marcy were gone, he would have said to himself, "I definitely don't feel good about my financial past."

For some of you, this story may have many similarities to your life. For others, this may look nothing like your current reality; that is always the danger of using examples. You may be older or younger, female not male, make more money or less money. You may be a business owner and have never worked for a corporation a day in your life. Or you might have worked for multiple companies in your career (and probably have.) You might not have a matching provision for your 401(k). As a matter of fact, you might not even have a 401(k) – but that's okay! You will face the same potentially devastating tax disasters unless you choose a better way!

In this book, I will show you there *is* a better way to save money for your future. A simple way. A way that you don't feel like your money is being held captive until retirement age. A way that you can get at your money *any time* and in *any amount* without paying any taxes ... that's right ... *zero!* A way that does not hold you hostage to the changing tax rates of the future. And a way to live a fully-funded retirement, enjoying all the things you want to do and still leaving behind a potentially huge legacy that will pass to the next generation free from federal and state income tax.

13

Retirement Trap #1 – The Tax Trap

Remember, Bill's story may be nothing like your own. You may be single. Or you may be married with no kids. You may make $30,000 a year. Or you may make $300,000 a year. You may be a corporate executive. Or you may run a small business out of your home. It really doesn't matter. What does matter is that you understand all the issues at play in this story, because they effect *you* in the same manner.

In these next four chapters I'd like to explore the dangers that lie beneath the surface of the obvious. Dangers that could potentially destroy the financial golden years of your life. Dangers that I have named the *Retirement Traps*.

To begin, let's look at the make-up of most people's retirement account once they reach retirement age. Do you think most of their accumulated savings is contribution or gain? If you said gain, you'd be correct ... by a wide margin.

Let's look at some real numbers to see just how significant this really is. If someone were to contribute only $100 a month into a retirement account over a 30-year period, that person would have contributed $36,000. If we project a 10% growth rate into the future, that $36,000 would have grown into a whopping $226,049 – a 528% total return!

If this individual had been contributing to a tax-qualified retirement plan they would have delayed (not saved) the tax on their $36,000 contribution. Generally speaking, an individual's net taxable income will be lowest in the early years of their career, not just because they are earning less, but also because they generally have the most tax deductions – the two major deductions being mortgage interest and children in the home. So even if someone is a fairly high income earner, their *net* tax rate might end up being as low as 15-20% due to the effect of itemized write-offs. And if they own their own business, it is likely lower than that.

So let's calculate the current tax delay (not savings) for the individual who contributed $36,000, using a 20% net tax rate, just to be conservative. Twenty percent of $36,000 is a total tax deferral (not savings) of $7,200 during all the accumulation years.

Well now, that's not bad. We would all like to save $7,200. But let's not forget, that tax was never saved; it was just delayed.

As we mentioned, if we apply a 10% growth rate to this savings, this individual would end up with around $226,049 in their retirement account. Though we don't know what tax rate this individual can expect to pay at retirement (and we will address this later), we do know that they have likely lost their primary tax deductions.

A primary goal for many retirees is to own their house debt-free. They don't want a mortgage payment chipping away at their retirement income. Therefore, many retired people no longer have the benefit of a mortgage deduction on their income tax. At the same time, since their children are grown and have moved out (hopefully), they also do not have the benefit of claiming their children as dependents. The net effect? Fewer tax deductions. And fewer tax deductions translate into a higher *net* tax rate.

Before we look at the probable tax scenario this individual will face in retirement, we need to make an assumption; we need to guess what this individual's *net* tax rate will be in retirement. For simplicity, let's be generous and assume the same low net tax rate of only 20% in retirement. If we apply that rate to the total balance of the tax-qualified plan, you get a whopping tax liability of $45,210. Ouch! That doesn't sound very appealing. So much for the benefits of the $7,200 tax deferral. That deferral just cost the individual nearly seven times more in actual taxes to be paid over the life of withdrawals from their account. And the death-tax picture is even worse.

The reality, however, is that the net tax rate in retirement will often be *higher* than the net tax during the accumulation years, even if an individual's gross income is exactly the same, or even less. Again, this is due to the loss of some key tax write-offs that were available earlier. In reality, this individual's net tax rate could easily be 30% to 40%, especially if they live in a state with a moderately high state income tax. If the net tax rate was 30%, then the total tax liability would be $67,815 instead of the $45,210. At 40%, the tax liability jumps to $90,419.

Would any of us really trade $45,210, $67,815, or $90,419 for a *delay* of paying a small $7,200? No, of course not! But, unfortunately, that is what millions of Americans are doing every day as they contribute to their tax-qualified plans. And remember, these numbers are based on the small savings of only $100 per month. If a person were to save $1,000 per month, or more, as allowed by most tax-qualified plans, then the problem becomes *ten times* worse. That appealing deduction on taxes today might end up costing $450,210, $670,815, or $900,419, or more.

What people fail to realize is that tax-qualified plans <u>*do not avoid tax, they simply delay tax. And by delaying tax, these*</u>

plans compound tax, making the tax burden worse – much, much worse.

Step back for a minute and consider whose retirement you are planning? Is there any question why the government promotes tax-qualified programs? Uncle Sam is building *his* retirement at *your* expense.

In chapter nineteen, I am going to show you how you can pay the $7,200 tax on your contribution today, but then withdraw your entire $226,049 account tax-free. Not just tax-delayed, but *tax-free.*

As we look at the next issue regarding taxation, let me ask you a critical question. Do you believe future taxes will be higher or lower than they are today? Think about this for moment. In the course of writing this book, I asked this question frequently to get a gauge of the public's opinion of future taxation. And guess what? Every person, without fail, told me they expected to pay higher taxes in the future. I fully agree.

Think about what we are facing as a country. We have undertaken a massive and costly war on terrorism. Who's going to pay that bill? We have heard about a renewed commitment to space exploration. Who's going to pay that bill? And we have all recently experienced the devastating hurricanes that ravaged the southeast. And still I ask the question, who's going to pay that bill?

The answer to all three questions is – you. You the American taxpayer. Please know I am not editorializing on any of the above items. You may be one who agrees with these expenditures, or you may be one who disagrees with them. It really doesn't matter. You are still going to pay the bill. And while these are some large and immediate expenses that will affect the economy and the national budget for years to come, I believe there are three even more daunting issues lingering on the horizon that must be addressed to prevent a potential national financial collapse.

The first of these issues is our failing Social Security system. Soon there will be one worker supporting every retired person. And don't think for a second that your Social Security contributions are sitting in a nice little account for you to access someday. They're not. No, they are already spent. Every penny of them. It's a pay as you go system that is on the brink of disaster. If you don't believe me, go pull out your last Social Security statement. On the right side of the front page read the words carefully,

"About Social Security's future…

"For more than 60 years, America has kept the promise of security for its workers and their families. But now, the Social Security system is facing serious future financial problems, and action is needed soon to make sure that the system is sound when today's younger workers are ready for retirement.

"Today, there are almost 36 million Americans age 65 or older. Their Social Security retirement benefits are funded by today's workers and their employers who jointly pay Social Security taxes – just as the money they paid into Social Security was used to pay benefits to those who retired before them. ***Unless action is taken soon to strengthen Social Security, in just 14 years we will begin paying more in benefits than we collect in taxes. Without changes, by 2042 the Social Security Trust Fund will be exhausted.*** [Bold and underline by author.] By then the number of Americans 65 or older is expected to have doubled. There won't be enough younger people working to pay all of the benefits owed to those who are retiring. At that point, there will be enough money to pay only about 73 cents for each dollar of scheduled benefits."[6]

Why do you think the government printed these words on the front page of the Social Security statement and began sending them out to every worker, every year? Is it because they know of the coming disaster and they want to cover their own backsides?

Though most Americans don't read these statements and do not know this pending disaster even exists, the government wants the liability to be back on us as individuals so no one can ever say, "No one ever told me I wasn't going to have a Social Security benefit!" All the government has to say is, "We told you so every year for the last 30 years. Don't blame us!"

On January 11, 2005, President Bush made the following remarks at Andrew W. Mellon Auditorium in Washington, DC, "Now, I readily concede some would say, well, it's [Social Security] not bankrupt yet; why don't we wait until it's bankrupt? The problem with that notion is that the longer you wait, the more difficult it is to fix. You realize that this system of ours is going to be short the difference between obligation and money coming in, by about $11 trillion, unless we act. And that's an issue. That's trillion with a 'T.'"

What? An eleven *TRILLION*-dollar shortfall? How can that be possible? That's nearly 38% *more* than our total national debt.

On January 13, 2005, Vice President Cheney echoed the president's remarks at Catholic University. "Again, the projected shortfall in Social Security exceeds $10 trillion; that figure is nearly twice the combined wages and salaries of every single working American last year."

Whoa!

In reality, I don't believe the government will let Social Security fail, because it would have a public uprising on its hands unlike America has ever seen; but to keep the program viable, it has only one option – higher taxes!

The second reason I believe we will face future taxes much higher than today is due to our immense national debt. It has spiraled out of control and now stands at an unimaginable $8,554,808,534,095 (over eight and a half trillion dollars) as of October 2006 according to the U.S National Debt Clock, and it is increasing at approximately $1.6 billion per day. To put this in perspective, every one of the 300 million Americans alive in this country today would have to contribute $28,511 in order to pay this off.[7] That includes every man, woman, child, and infant alive in America today. With it growing at an unprecedented rate, this mammoth mountain may already be insurmountable. At some point, however, this will need to be addressed. And there are only two ways to address it. Spend less. Collect more. Do you hear what I hear? Higher taxes!

Before I move on to my third reason that I believe we will see higher taxes in the future, I want to pause a moment on the issue of our national debt. As I was researching our country's debt for this chapter, what began as measured concern grew into a red-alert alarm of catastrophic proportions. Our debt is out of control. It was less than three years ago, in December 2003, that our debt stood at $7 trillion. What does that mean? In less than three years, the debt has grown by over $1,500,000,000,000 – one and a half TRILLION dollars. In three short years!

Let me put this into its overwhelming perspective. Back in 1791, yes 215 years ago, our national debt stood at $75,463,476 – a little above seventy-five million dollars. However, forty-four years later, in 1835, our national debt had been reduced to a mere $33,733. Essentially, we were nearly debt-free as a nation. From this date forward, our debt has been on a steady and atmospheric rise. So in a period of 168 years (1835-2003) we managed to amass $7 trillion in debt. The extra $1.5 trillion we have tacked on in the last three years represents a whopping 17% of the *total debt* it has taken us 171 years to accumulate. Think about that for a moment. Seventeen percent of our total national debt has occurred in the last three years, or approximately 1% of the total time involved incurring this debt. Are things speeding up? Absolutely! Do you think this will slow down? No way!

Unless debts get paid down, the debt snowball continues to grow bigger and bigger and move faster and faster. We're staring at a snowball the size of Mt. Everest. How much larger can this snowball get before we all get buried under the largest financial avalanche in the world's history?

Do you remember the story of Mr. Interest? Well, he's working night and day to do his best to cripple the future of our economy; and I fear he just might succeed.

One other interesting fact I discovered, that may have eluded you the same mysterious way it eluded me, is that in October 2004 we as a nation had reached our predetermined borrowing cap of $7.38 trillion. Did you know that? I didn't. So, did the government do what you and I would do if we had maxed out all our lines of credit? Did they stop spending? Of course not. Did they shut down government or reduce the number of individuals on the public payroll? Not that I'm aware of. What did they do? On November 17, 2004:

> "A divided Senate approved an $800 billion increase in the federal debt limit.... The 52-44 vote, mostly along party lines, was expected to be followed by House passage today. Enactment would raise the government's borrowing limit to $8.18 trillion – more than eight times the total federal debt that existed when President Reagan took office in 1981."[8]

What did they do? They raised their debt ceiling and borrowed more. Congress is forced to continue this disastrous debt cycle, or our country's fragile house of cards will come tumbling down, likely bringing the world economy with it.

To prove this true, let me quote another article from March 16, 2006, *a mere 16 months after the previous article*, entitled, "Congress Sets new Federal Debt Limit: $9 Trillion." Wasn't it

Yogi Berra who said, "This is déjà vu all over again." Well, if the shoe fits ....

"Federal debt has risen from $542 billion to more than $8 trillion since 1975. Debt as a percentage of Gross Domestic product, once at 34.7%, is now above 60%.

Faced with a potential government shutdown, the Senate votes to raise the nation's debt limit for the fourth time in five years. The bill passed by a 52-48 vote, increasing the ceiling to $9 trillion. The bill now goes to the president.

The debt now stands at more than $8.2 trillion.

Like many cash-strapped Americans who have maxed-out credit cards, the federal government has hit its limit for borrowing funds to keep operating. If the limit isn't raised, the government likely will run out of borrowing authority within days, risking a shutdown.

When President Bush took office five years ago, the national debt was at $5.6 trillion; since then, big budget surpluses have collapsed into huge deficits, and the debt has shot up nearly 50 percent."[9]

I believe it is clearer than ever that the only way we are going to survive as a nation will be significantly higher tax burdens on everyone in the years and decades to come; the bills need to be paid because the alternative is unspeakable.

The third reason I believe we will see higher tax rates in the future is due to a potential inferno that is just past the initial stages of ignition – the rising cost of health care in America. The costs are out of control as individuals are living longer and demanding more services and more prescription drugs than ever before. Lump on top of that the lack of litigation control and you have the recipe for future disaster.

It is my personal opinion, as well as the view of many of my friends in the health care industry, that the eventual result in America will be similar to that in other developed countries – a government-run health care program. The funding vehicle once again will have to be higher taxes for Americans!

However, even if the government doesn't formally take over the *entire* health care system, think what is happening to our population. It is aging rapidly. Baby boomers are reaching retirement age in record numbers. And what health care plan are *all* American citizens on at the age of 65? Medicare. <u>Tax-funded health care!</u> In other words, we are going to have an increasing number of individuals on government-sponsored health care one way or another. People will continue to live longer, which will result in the need for more medical care at older ages. This will be further exacerbated by the increasing availability and life-prolonging effects of new prescription drug technology, again adding even more years to our already increasing life span. And as you can guess, there is only one logical way to pay for this increased demand for medical care services by a growing elderly population – higher taxes!

Though this is merely a cursory list of the issues we face that could drive up taxes in the future, one thing I believe is true, Americans will be faced with much larger tax rates in the decades ahead.

So, if this is indeed the case, would you rather pay your taxes now or later? Not only can you pay tax on a much smaller *amount* now, but you can do so at potentially lower tax *rates*, thus compounding your savings effect. The other option is to have your entire nest-egg taxed at potentially astronomical rates in the future.

* * *

I do need to pause at this point and point out to you one issue that this book is not taking into consideration – and for good reason. I realize that if you deposit money this year into a tax-qualified retirement plan, you will receive a tax savings in the current year. If you were to reinvest that savings into some other financial vehicle each and every year, it would allow you to save more money currently than you would otherwise be able to do with an after-tax vehicle. Some folks in the financial world may take issue with the fact that I am silent on this point; however, I am not ignoring it out of ignorance.

The reason this book does not address this issue is because I believe it is irrelevant. In all my years I have rarely, if ever, seen anyone save the difference. They may fully intend to, mind you, but it just doesn't happen. It's America, for goodness sake. We know how to spend. As a matter of fact, the money is usually spent before we have earned it. It is my experience that if someone is realizing a savings on their tax-qualified retirement plan, it will not become additional savings but will rather be assimilated into an already over-stretched budget.

14

Retirement Trap #2 – The Access Trap

Why do you think most Americans plan to retire around the ages of sixty or sixty-five? Is it coincidence that these dates usually coincide with the year the individual has access to either their Social Security or to their tax-qualified retirement plan?

As a bit of an aside, I believe the entire concept of retirement has been spoon-fed to the American public by the government and by financial planners for so long that few individuals ever stop to ask a few basic questions. Why do I want to retire? If I do plan to retire, why am I choosing the age at which I will do so? What am I going to spend the rest of my life doing?

A friend of mine who retired a few years ago after serving as a corporate executive for decades shared with me some interesting insights. He said, "Patrick, people did a great job of helping me set up my finances for retirement. Actually, that was quite simple. No one, however, helped me prepare my *life* for this next season. I knew this date was coming for years, but I never really spent time thinking about what I would do, how I would spend my time, or what I would pursue next."

I believe a lot of people have set a retirement date in the future simply because … because 59 ½ is when they can get at their tax-qualified retirement account … because 65 is when they can get social security … because, because, because, because, because … sounds like a song from the Wizard of Oz.

I would like to see people separate their desire for retirement from the access to their money. The plan I am going to show you will do this. Fully. Completely. But for now, let's explore *Trap #2 – The Access Trap.*

Remember our friend Bill? How much was it going to cost him to access money from his 401(k) to help fund his daughter's college education? Since Bill was still working and earning a good income, all money pulled out of his retirement plan had to be added to his existing income, sending him into the highest marginal tax bracket very quickly. Let's assume that marginal tax bracket to be 40% – only slightly higher than today's rate in 2006. He also has a 10% state tax and a 10% early withdrawal tax penalty. Therefore, Bill has to fork over 60 cents of every dollar to the IRS to pull money out of his retirement account before age 59 ½. Sixty cents!

So to fund his daughter's $77,356 tuition (which unfortunately is likely to be what a year of private school tuition will cost in the year 2018), Bill would have to withdraw $193,390 in actual dollars and then cough up $116,034 of that to Uncle Sam. Who in their right mind would do that? No one.

Can you see why Bill was frustrated? Can you see why he felt his money was being held hostage? I certainly would feel this way, and so would you.

In basic terms, *The Access Trap* is simple. Your money is not really your own, at least not until you meet the government's eligibility guidelines. But don't forget that even when you avoid the 10% tax penalty, you are still crushed by the potential 45% (or higher) income tax (federal and state) that can and will still be due.

When you step back and see this reality in black and white, it really does sound a bit criminal, doesn't it?

One of the questions people ask me every time they hear about this new retirement concept is, "Why isn't everyone doing this?"

I look back at them and say, "The only reason I can think of why everyone isn't taking advantage of this strategy is because most people have never heard about this concept before. Think about yourself. Before today had you ever heard about this idea?"

"No," they reply.

"Well," I continue, "Everyone else is just like you. Quite frankly, I have been working in this industry for fifteen years and very few of my colleagues in the financial world even understand the full benefit of this strategy themselves. And there's a reason for that. You see, the product that allows you to overcome all the traps of the tax-qualified plan is offered only by insurance companies; and unfortunately, most insurance agents are not very well trained in the financial realm. They are uncomfortable talking about money and don't really feel this is an area they want to help people manage. They like managing risk, not money.

"Conversely, most stock brokers and money managers don't offer insurance products; and if they do, they generally don't understand the first thing about them and don't want to.

"Therefore, the agents who offer the potential solution to this problem don't fully understand its advantage and the people who manage most of the wealth in this country don't like or understand insurance products. It's a classic Catch 22, and the customer is stuck right in the middle."

It is my desire that this book, *Tax-Free Retirement*, will bridge this gap and shatter the glass ceiling that has held the public back from the most advantageous wealth accumulation and distribution tool that, in my opinion, has ever existed.

As we conclude this chapter, let me leave you with some final questions to ponder about *The Access Trap*. Do you really want to sock all your long-term savings away into an account that for all intents and purposes can't be touched? Wouldn't it be better if you had full access to your money at *any time* and at *any age*? Might you adjust your retirement plans if that were the case? Maybe you would work the job you are currently in until the age of 50 and then pursue one of your life-long dreams. Would you write the book you've always wanted? Would you start the business you've always pondered? Would you take up flying lessons, travel, work part-time, or volunteer in your community?

If you had access to your retirement savings at any age, you would be freed up to take a step backward in earned income. Slow down. Take a break. Take a sabbatical. Work three days a week. Pursue your dreams. Enjoy your kids. Dote on your grandkids. You name it, because it would be *your* choice. And these choices would be available to you at any age, assuming you had saved enough money to provide an adequate income.

You might find you love your new occupation so much that you never plan to retire because you are finally pursuing your life's dream. You are energized. You're full of life. More life than you have ever experienced.

And if you find that you love your new occupation so much that you are going to keep working well into your twilight years, and it is providing the necessary income to meet your living expenses, you could let the savings in your nest egg continue to grow indefinitely. If you utilize these strategies, there is no age in which you are forced to begin taking income. You can let it grow and accumulate for some exciting possibilities.

Once again, this is *not* the case with tax-qualified retirement plans. Not only is there a *Tax Trap* and an *Access Trap*, but an often overlooked trap that many individuals don't know exists is *The Distribution Trap*. Let's explore.

15

Retirement Trap #3 – The Distribution Trap

This is going to be a short chapter because the *Distribution Trap* is relatively simple to understand. Yes, there are many laws and rulings that determine how it actually plays out for the individual, but I often find that less is more.

All you need to know about *The Distribution Trap* is how it works and how it can affect your future.

In simple terms, the IRS wants to get *its* hands on *its* retirement. Sure, the account may have your name on it, but when thirty, forty, or even fifty percent of your distribution can go to the bureaucratic coffers, you have to step back and wonder, "Whose retirement is this anyway?"

Here's how it works. By April 1st after the year you reach the age of 70 ½ you *must* begin taking a distribution from your tax-qualified retirement account, whether that is a 401(k), a Traditional IRA, a SEP, a SIMPLE, or any other type of qualified retirement plan. The government provides guidelines on how much this distribution must be each year, and it varies by a number of different factors. There are many free Web sites that provide calculators for individuals to estimate the amount that is needed to be withdrawn; however, not to worry, the company that manages your plan will be responsible for notifying you as to the amount which you are required to take.

So what happens if you don't take this mandatory distribution? Well, I'd like you to read it straight from IRS Publication 590 for the 2003 tax year. (This is referring specifically to a traditional IRA, but by the time an individual is 70 ½ that's most likely where their money will be. I'll explain why after we look at the quote from the IRS publication.) It reads:

> "You cannot keep amounts in your traditional IRA indefinitely. Generally, you must begin receiving distributions by April 1 of the year following the year in which you reach age 70½. The required minimum distribution for any year after the year in which you reach age 70½ must be made by December 31 of that later year.
>
> ***Tax on excess.*** If distributions are less than the required minimum distribution for the year, discussed earlier under *When Must You Withdraw Assets? (Required Minimum Distributions)*, you may have to pay a 50% excise tax for that year on the amount not distributed as required."[10]

The reason this rule affects just about everyone is because once a person retires they often have to (and generally choose to) roll their tax-qualified money into a new, self-directed Traditional IRA. Why? Because they are no longer officially associated with their prior company and either the company won't allow them to continue or they want to control the financial decisions themselves. But, even if they are one of the few individuals that can keep their money in their existing plan, and they choose to do so, it really doesn't matter, because the *laws of distribution for other tax-qualified plans are the same as they are for the IRA.*

So how do you feel about that excerpt from the IRS? Fifty percent excise tax! "That's got to be a joke," you say. Unfortunately, it's not. *They* are serious about getting *their* money.

So the looming question is, "If I don't need the money, do I still need to take the distribution?"

The answer is an unequivocal and resounding, "Yes!"

So let's review what we know so far about tax-qualified retirement plans.

Where is most retirement money today? In qualified retirement plans. To the tune of *trillions* of dollars.

Can I get my money out of my account before age 59 ½? No. At least not without a penalty. Under some special circumstances, you can, if you systematically liquidate your account over a number of years, but for all intents and purposes you cannot.

If I do take money out before age 59 ½, what happens? On top of the substantial tax you would normally have to pay, you also incur an additional 10% penalty tax.

After I reach the age of 59 ½, can I get my money out tax-free? Sorry, no again. Every penny in your tax-qualified account (including your original contributions) will be taxed at your current tax bracket at the *time of withdrawal.*

What if I don't need the money in retirement? Can I let it accrue in my account and pass it along to my heirs? Once again, no. Regardless of whether you need the money or not, you must begin withdrawing it in the year after you reach age 70 ½.

What about at death? How does this account get taxed? Glad you asked. That's Retirement Trap #4 – *The Death Trap.* If you thought the others three traps were bad, wait until you understand this one.

16

Retirement Trap #4 – The Death Trap

The Titanic was a great ship. It was the grandest the world had ever seen. It had only one small problem – it didn't make it to its destination. With all its lavish décor and advanced engineering, it couldn't do what even the relatively primitive sailing ships of Columbus had done more than 400 years before.

Why? Why didn't the Titanic make it to its destination? The answer is simple – it hit an iceberg.

Have you ever thought what would happen if you hit an iceberg? Not literally like the Titanic, but figuratively. You see, the Titanic's experience is not too far from that of our own everyday lives. We have icebergs lurking in our waters. Financial Icebergs. Sickness Icebergs. Accident Icebergs. Catastrophe Icebergs. Each one eager to sink and destroy. Eager to send us plummeting to the depths, broken and tattered. Eager to keep us from our destination.

For those of you participating in tax-qualified retirement plans, have you ever thought what would happen if you hit the granddaddy of all icebergs – the Death Iceberg? What if you hit it tomorrow? What if you hit it in ten years? Maybe you won't hit it until a ripe old age. But know one thing; this is an iceberg you *will* hit. And when you do, what will be left behind for those you love and who love you?

So how does death affect the results of tax-qualified retirement plans? Let's take a look.

Death can present itself in two forms, expected and unexpected. During our lifetimes we have all probably experienced both. The phone call out of the blue telling us what we least want to hear. There's been an accident – unexpected.

As well, we have likely all sat by the bedside of someone who slowly slipped away from us after a long life of loving, warm memories – expected.

Eventually each of us will fall into one of those two categories – expected or unexpected – and when we do, *all* the decisions we have made during our life will leave ripples in the waters of those left behind.

Let's look at just one of those decisions. The decision to use a tax-qualified retirement plan.

Iceberg #1 – Premature Death

When people sit down with their financial planners or their company's plan administrator to talk about retirement planning what picture do you think they have in mind?

I can tell you because I sit with these same people every day. They picture themselves at some golden age in the distant future, on the golf course, sipping Mai Tai's in Maui, traveling the world, visiting their grandkids, serving their community. Something. Anything. What they don't picture is dying tomorrow.

Their picture of the future extends way beyond tomorrow. Quite frankly, it usually extends way beyond the next decade. Most individuals don't stop long enough to ask the all important question, "What if my future is only tommorow?"

That is the question that none of us likes to face. We somehow feel it is too morbid. So what do we do instead? We ignore it. We pretend the reality of premature death doesn't exist. And as we go through life pretending this reality doesn't exist, we make decisions that rip apart the lives of those we love and leave behind – destruction as equally devastating as those who went down on the great ship, Titanic.

Would it have been too morbid for the engineers of the Titanic to ask a similar question, "What happens if this ship hits an iceberg?"

Of course not. Not only is this *not* a morbid question, you would be angry if that question hadn't been considered. It's called planning.

The reason I have spent so much time laying this foundation is because the lack of planning for premature death has led people to make a common and critical financial error. They don't leave enough money for those left behind.

This lack of money can occur two ways. First, because an individual's savings has not had the power of compound interest or time, it is a fraction of that future nest egg. For example, if a person were able to put $1,000 per month into their tax-qualified plan, they could possibly expect to build a nest egg north of $3,000,000 in thirty years, a reasonable saving period for a working individual. And it's that number that sticks in their brain. It's that number that fuels their retirement dreams.

But what if all that is stopped short? What if they hit an iceberg? What if they make one monthly deposit into their plan and then find themselves the victim of premature death? Their account stands at the value of their deposit, a whopping total of $1,000. Even if the unexpected didn't happen for five years, their account still sits at a number far less than $100,000 – hardly enough to fund a family's needs or a spouse's future.

Secondly, the other way this lack of money gets played out is not enough life insurance. In my fifteen years in the insurance industry I have *never, not even one time*, met with an individual who has had adequate life insurance in place prior to our meeting. Think about that for a moment. I have met with hundreds of people and not once has a person actually had a sufficient amount of death benefit. That example by itself should be enough proof that people don't like to face the reality of premature death.

I could expound on all the reasons why this is probably the case, but I believe they boil down to the same two reasons we have already discussed – 1) People don't think premature death will really happen to them, and/or 2) People greatly underestimate how much money it will really take to provide for the loved ones they leave behind.

During my career, my calculations have consistently shown that it takes somewhere between seven to ten times an annual income in liquid cash to properly protect a family. Since most people don't have this amount sitting around in a bank or investment account, that leaves the bulk of the burden to rest on the shoulders of life insurance.

But how much life insurance do people actually have? My experience shows somewhere between one to three times their incomes. A sizeable shortage to say the least.

Before I leave you completely discouraged, I want to give you the good news. Don't dispair. Take hope. In the next chapter, I am going to give you the answer that will render the iceberg of premature death obsolete, at least in regard to your finances and the future of your loved ones. If you follow my plan, you can remove that iceberg from your financial waters forever. But before you skip ahead to the solution, please carefully read the next section, because there is an equally daunting iceberg that still lurks below the water line, waiting to put a hole in your financial ship. Keep going, you're almost there.

Iceberg #2 – Expected Death

Hopefully, you will find yourself in the majority of the population and experience a long, full life. Hopefully the golden years will be just that – golden.

If that is the case, then all your planning and saving has been a worthy undertaking that will now fuel the dreams you have pondered so long. It's time to enjoy the fruits of your labor.

However, I do not think the proper vision of retirement is one of lethargy and laziness, a time to stop working; rather, a great vision of retirement is one for increased investment, not financial, but relational. A time for increased investment in your spouse, if you have one. A time to share your wisdom with the next generation. A time to volunteer at civic organizations that so desperately need help. Yes, retirement can be the richest of all seasons in life. No wonder it is called the golden age.

However, all this relational investment takes time, and as the old adage goes, time is money.

If you have saved diligently in your tax-qualified retirement plan then you have accrued a sum of money to help pay the bills. Hopefully you have saved enough to pay *all* the bills. But regardless, I have found one thing to be universally true with good savers. They remain good savers in retirement. This may sound hard to believe, but it is incredibly hard to begin *spending* the money that you have spent so long accumulating. To become a consumer of your retirement monies requires a drastic change in your thinking. And many people don't make the switch easily.

One other reality retirees face is the fact that their savings have to last for their entire lifetimes. The difficulty of that proposition is that no one knows just how long they are going to live. My grandmother just turned eighty-nine, and if you ask her about her future, she will tell you it is bright and long. She believes she has a decade or more in front of her, and she just might.

So people figure out very quickly that even if they do start spending their retirement money, they need to be careful and conserve it so that it lasts longer then they do. One method of stretching out money that I have frequently seen practiced is for retirees to only spend the growth, or interest, in their account, leaving their original nest egg intact. This gives them comfort and provides the security they desire. For some, this will provide enough income to live their dreams, for most it won't. But in almost all cases I have discovered one thing. There is almost always money left in the account at the retiree's death. Often *lots* of money!

Please note my next statement, because it is one of the most important statements I will make in this book. ***The single worst place to have money at death is in a tax-qualified account.***

Why? What happens to money left in a tax-qualified plan at the time of death? Let me tell you, it's not pretty. As a matter of fact, it's downright ugly.

Tax-qualified plans get treated differently, depending on whether the money is passing to a living spouse or not. If the retiree is married, then the account will pass to the spouse with no taxation issues. However, if the retiree is not married or has been predeceased by his or her spouse, then the account gets absolutely obliterated by taxes. Likewise, if the tax-qualified plan is passed to a living spouse, the account will get similarly devastated at the death of the second spouse. So there is no escape. Let me describe the pending disaster.

As you are certainly aware, the Federal tax rates are broken into different percentages based on varying income bands. In 2006 the Federal income tax brackets look like this:[11]

Single	Married – Joint Return	Married Separate Return	Marginal Tax Rate
$0	$0	$0	10%
$7,551	$15,101	$7,551	15%
$30,651	$61,301	$30,651	25%
$74,201	$123,701	$61,851	28%
$154,801	$188,451	$94,226	33%
$336,550	$336,550	$168,275	35%

When you are talking about a person's life savings, it really doesn't take much to accumulate an account worth more than $350,000.

Read these next words very carefully. *At death (except if passing to a spouse) the entire account gets treated as taxable income paid in that year and gets taxed at the appropriate tax rate.* Do you see what that means? Can you tell how that will impact your account?

Let's put some numbers to it. It is in no way uncommon to see $1,000,000, $2,000,000, or even $3,000,000 or more left in a tax-qualified plan at the participant's death. Remember, most retirees don't want to spend down the principle in their account, because they don't want the money to run out before they do.

At today's top tax rate, a $1,000,000 account would get hit with $350,000 in federal income tax and $90,000 in state income tax (if you live in a state with a 9% income tax.) That's a whopping $440,000 vaporized immediately. And not to beat a dead horse, but if marginal tax rates rise (which I believe will be a necessity in the future), that 35% could go to 50%, 55%, 60%, or higher.

As ridiculous as that may seem to you, I think the government could sell those tax rates to the public quite easily, making them believe they are not affected. In reality, it would be the biggest scam of the century. Here's why.

Every time there is a tax debate, one of the political parties pushes to lower tax rates for the lower and middle class, while raising taxes only on the wealthy. Many Americans believe that sounds reasonable. They think, "Hey, I'm not one of those rich Americans so what do I care. Stick it to 'em! They can afford to pay the taxes."

So, let's say in the future some administration proposed to have a top marginal tax rate of 55%, but only on those who make more than $1,000,000 per year. They would show the statistics that something like .05% of Americans fall into that category, so it would affect very few individuals. The public would buy it because it wouldn't affect them. Or would it?

Indeed it would, for the reason previously discussed. America would be duped. It would be the con of the century. It would foster one of the largest wealth transfers in history, but the transfer would flow one direction – right into Uncle Sam's pockets.

As we have discussed, we are approaching the largest bubble of retirees and consequently retirement monies in history. Many middle class Americans will accumulate retirement savings in excess of $1,000,000. If these new tax rates were to be enacted, then instead of $440,000 being paid in tax at death, it could now be $640,000. It is conceivable that 64% of a tax-qualified account could be paid in tax upon their death. Immediately. Permanently.

An issue I'm not even beginning to address in the scope of this book is the estate tax, or "death tax," as derided by opponents. Trying to predict what that might look like decades in the future is like using a slingshot to try and hit an F-17 at 40,000 feet. We know the rules through 2011, but after that it is all back to the drawing board. If the sunset provision in the estate tax code were to set back the clock (which it is set to do), then it is likely that there would be additional tax on top of the federal and state taxes we illustrated in the last example. But for now, we'll ignore this piece, because it's not critical to the discussion at hand.

Even without estate tax, do you really want to take the chance of having Uncle Sam be a 64% heir to your retirement account? It could be more; it could be less. But what if you could cut Uncle Sam out altogether? How would that feel?

Do you see why a change in the marginal tax rates doesn't effect just the wealthy?

Would you really like to save money all your life knowing that the *majority* stakeholder (much more than 50%) at retirement will be the government? If you could choose who received that money, would the first person on your list be the IRS? Certainly not. Who would you give it to? Your kids? A charity? An alma mater? Your favorite niece or nephew? When you stop to think about it, you'd give it to anybody before you gave it to the government.

If you have money in a tax-qualified plan at death, you're stuck! Uncle Sam is going to get his cut – and he can hardly wait.

Like I promised, we are finally there. In this next chapter I am going to show you how you can fix this problem. I'm going to show how you can give your money *to any person or any organization totally and completely income-tax free.* Uncle Sam won't see a penny, at least in income tax.

Wouldn't you much rather have your money in an account that you control? An account that lets you get at your money any time you want. An account that can cost you *zero* in taxes when you take your money out - if done properly. An account that you can leave the money in for as long as you want. An account in which you can direct who receives the full balance at your death. And an account that will pass totally income-tax free to whomever you designate at your death. I don't know about you, but that's my kind of account.

The groundwork has been set. Let's see how you can create this kind of account for yourself.

Part IV: The Retirement Solution

17

The Retirement Solution – The Basic Foundation

I have found that part of the reason people often miss the very best in life is that they hold misconceptions and falsehoods closely as truth. It may be because of a parent or a teacher, a book or a television show, but somewhere along the line people create a series of truths that become inviolable, but in fact, are completely false.

Think of some of those things in your own life. Did a parent tell you as a child that if you went to bed with wet hair you'd catch a cold? You certainly believed it at the time. Do you now? More than likely. What about, "if you pull out a gray hair ten more will grow back?" It's quite humorous the things we hold true because someone simply stated it as fact. We trusted the person, so we never researched the issue ourselves. We never did our own homework. It simply became our reality, and we propagated it as truth to others as well, without so much as even a shred of proof.

When I tell you the solution to all of the problems we have raised so far in this book, you may have a negative initial reaction.

You might find the voice of some previous financial advisor or book or talk show host whispering in your ear. It's possible you might have a very strong reaction. Why do I know this? For two reasons. First, I had that type of reaction myself; and secondly, so do many of the people I visit with.

When I ask them *why* they believe what they do, they cannot produce an answer. That is because they're not really sure why they believe what they do. Their usual answer is along the line of, "I don't know. Someone told me that once." Until our visit, they have never looked into the truth or figured it out for themselves. They simply heard a statement somewhere along the line that they have held true for years.

So what is the solution to preparing financially for retirement? It is this. *It is my belief that the single best place to save retirement dollars is in a permanent life insurance contract.*

Did you have that reaction? Did you hear the voices? You may say, "But that can't be true!" With all the jazzed up financial products on the market, how in the world can life insurance be the best place for long term savings and wealth accumulation? Isn't life insurance about dying?

Let me start this new journey with a simple but profound explanation of how life insurance works. This basis is the foundation upon which we will build the rest of our understanding. Pretend you are sitting across from me at my desk. Let me guide you through one of the most powerful revelations you will ever experience in the financial realm. Here we go...

In this world there are only two kinds of insurance. Yes, you will hear many different names, 10-year term, second to die, executive benefit life, 20-year term, 30-year term, whole life, graded premium life, decreasing term, universal life, etc., etc., etc. Every company has its own names and its own variations. But know this; there are only two kinds of life insurance – term and permanent.

Each of these products has four unique characteristics. As I explain these characteristics, I want you to consider an analogy. Think of term insurance like *renting* a home and permanent insurance like *buying* a home. As we go through, I think you'll find amazing similarities.

I'll start with term insurance. The first characteristic of term insurance is that it is *low cost – initially* ... just like renting a home is cheaper than buying a home. Right?

The second characteristic of term insurance, however, is that the *premium goes up over time*. Each term policy is a little different, but at some point the premium *will* go up, just like rent on a home. You may have signed a five-year lease with no increase in rents, but when the lease is done, what will likely happen? Rents will go up.

The third characteristic of term insurance is that is has *no equity*. Think about it. If you rented a home for ten years and then decided to move, how much of your rent payments would the landlord give back to you? None, except maybe a small damage deposit. All the money you paid over the years did one thing: it provided a place for you to live.

The fourth characteristic of term insurance, and the one I consider the most significant, is that at some point in the future, even if you are still alive, the coverage *will* end. For some policies it is age 80, 85, or 90. For many, it is a specified period of time, like at the end of ten or twenty years. But regardless of how long it runs, one thing is true – at least with every term policy I have ever seen – it has a drop dead point, even if *you* are still alive.

When do people need life insurance, at least the death benefit feature? The answer is simple – when they die. And when do most individuals die? The majority die when they are much older. Therefore, these term policies terminate right when they are most needed. Unfortunately, since most term policies get so expensive in the later years of life, most have been dropped long before they have run their course. So all that money (just like rent) has been thrown to the wind.

Now let's look at permanent insurance. The first characteristic of permanent insurance is that it has a *higher cost – initially.* Just like it is generally more expensive to buy a home then it is to rent a home.

Secondly, however, the *premium stays level.* It's designed not to go up in the later years. Think about your home mortgage. If you were to take out a traditional thirty-year fixed mortgage, how much will your payment go up during those thirty years? Zero. Your 360th payment is the same as your first, at least as far as the principle and interest is concerned. Let's look at a graph (figure 17.1) to compare how the different premiums might look. Let's say line "A" is the cost of term insurance and line "B" is the cost of permanent insurance. Line "B" begins much higher than line "A," but as you can see, it remains level. At some point in the future, line "A" (term insurance) will cost more, simply from an out-of-pocket expense standpoint, than line "B" (permanent insurance.) Just as it would cost you more out-of-pocket twenty years down the line to rent then it would if you had bought an equivalent home at the same time you started renting.

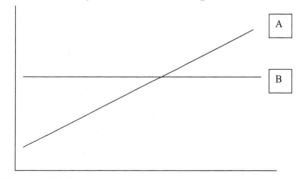

Figure 17.1

The third feature of permanent insurance is that it *builds equity*, just like owning a home. If you lived in your home for twenty years and then sold it, you would probably get back every dollar you paid for it and likely a lot more. The same is true with permanent insurance.

The fourth and final feature of permanent insurance is that the *coverage doesn't end*, as long as you pay the proper premium. With most quality permanent insurance there is not a predetermined date in the future where the coverage ceases to exist. It is designed to be there when you need it – hopefully much later in life.

So let's review one last time the four characteristics that differentiate term insurance from permanent insurance by looking at the chart below (figure 17.2):

Term Insurance	**Permanent Insurance**
1. Low cost – initially	1. Higher cost – initially
2. Cost goes up	2. Cost remains level
3. No equity	3. Builds Equity
4. Coverage ends	4. Coverage never ends

Figure 17.2

With that explanation, it appears that I hold a strong bias toward permanent insurance, and I must tell you – I do. However, I provide both kinds of insurance to my clients in equal proportion, because the one feature that both term and permanent similarly provide is a place to live – the death benefit. The most important issue in the life insurance discussion is the proper amount of coverage. If the amount of insurance that is needed can only be afforded through term insurance, then term it is.

However, if a person can afford the monthly (or annual) premium for permanent insurance, then just like being able to buy a home, permanent life insurance is by far the preferred option.

With that simple lesson, you now know more about life insurance than 90% of the rest of the world. Truly. Many insurance agents don't even fully understand these simple differences.

Though the issues just discussed are significantly important in the scope of a family's financial security, I have never met a person who has actually gotten excited figuring out the proper amount of death benefit. Many people see life insurance as a necessary evil. Many don't even see it as that. They avoid it all together.

I will guarantee one thing. The next few chapters will change your thinking about life insurance forever. Maybe it won't change your thinking about dealing with the death benefit portion, but you will find yourself, as silly as this may sound, thrilled about life insurance. You will see that life insurance can do far more than provide a death benefit. As a matter of fact, if structured properly, life insurance can serve as one of the most powerful retirement strategies available anywhere. I wouldn't be a bit surprised if you found yourself so excited about this new-found knowledge that you picked up the phone and set the first appointment available to get together with your insurance agent or the individual who gave you this book (if it was a life insurance agent or financial planner) to find out what specific options are best suited for you.

18

The Retirement Solution – Rules of Money

W hen you retire, you will have available to you only two kinds of money. Pots of money, I like to call them. The first pot of money is taxable and the second pot is tax-free. (See figure 18.1) Which pot would you like to have your money in? Taxable or tax-free?

In the taxable pot, you have two different types of taxation. The first kind is called capital-gains tax. This is the tax you pay for profit on things such as stocks, mutual funds, and real estate. There are two different tax levels within the capital gains structure. One is short-term capital-gains tax, which is applied to investments held shorter than a twelve-month period; this is usually taxed at the individual's marginal income-tax rate. The second tax level is for long-term holdings, investments held for greater than twelve months. The current capital gains tax (2006) on long-term holdings is generally 15%. But, of course, this is subject to change based on changes in the tax law.

On the other side of the taxable pot, we have income tax – the tax you are used to paying on the income you currently earn. The types of investments that are on this side of the taxable pot consist of all forms of tax-qualified plans and any other sources of earned income. This tax can be as high as 35% in 2006, but as we have discussed a few times, that number could easily go up in the future and probably will.

Now let's look at the other pot of money – the tax-free pot. Though there are three common places to accumulate tax-free income, only two, in my opinion, are viable enough to use as retirement savings vehicles. The three accumulation vehicles found inside of the tax-free pot are: 1) Municipal Bonds, 2) The Roth IRA,** 3) Life Insurance (if structured and managed properly – I'll elaborate later.)

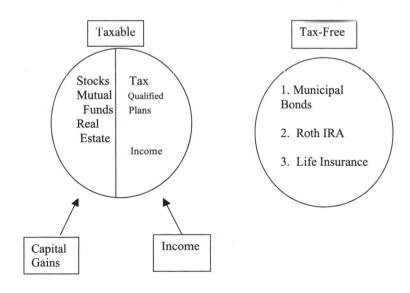

Figure 18.1

I disregard number one in the tax-free pot, municipal bonds, because over time they do not return enough nor provide the proper diversification to build a sufficient nest egg for retirement. So by eliminating number one, we are left with numbers two and three.

The Roth IRA is really a wonderful gift the government has given to us for retirement savings, but it only *begins* to do the job. Currently, an individual can put only $4,000 per year into a Roth IRA ($5,000 if they are age 50 and older). Though that number will certainly eek up over the years, it is still far short of what is needed to fund an adequate retirement living. The other major disadvantage is that high income earners can't participate. Once a combined household income reaches $150,000, the IRS begins to phase out how much can be contributed to a Roth IRA. Once the combined household income reaches $160,000 ($110,000 for a single person) the ability to contribute is eliminated altogether.

Once again, high-income earners are treated unfairly by the government. It makes no sense. But, that's the reality we have to live with.

So, if your household earns more than $160,000 per year ($110,000 for an unmarried individual), and you can't contribute to a Roth IRA, and municipal bonds don't provide an adequate savings venue, you are left with only one option in the tax-free pot. Life insurance. Luckily, this one remaining option is a fantastic one.

Remember, which pot of money do you want filled up when you retire? Taxable or tax-free? Tax-free of course.

Before we look at exactly how life insurance can properly provide this tax-free retirement strategy, I want to show you two more rules of money. The first rule of money is a very simple, ordered list I have named *The Smart Money Investment Order.* It's the order in which smart investment dollars should flow. Most people skip over the best options. I want you to be smarter than most people. See figure 18.2 below.

<u>*The Smart Money Investment Order*</u>
1. Free Money
2. Tax-Free Money
3. Tax-Deferred Money
4. Taxable Money

Figure 18.2

Let's look quickly at each one to determine what each means and how an investor could take advantage of it.

#1 – Free money! Sounds great, but how do I get it? Other than gifts from family or a planned inheritance, the only place I know in the business world to receive free money is through a matching program in a 401(k) or similar program at an individual's place of employment. Wait a minute, you say. The greater portion of this book has been spent explaining why employer sponsored retirement plans are *not* the best place to save for retirement. That is true – with one exception. Free money. I always encourage individuals to take advantage of all the free money they can get. In other words, I encourage them to contribute (if necessary) the *minimum* amount needed to maximize the free money that their company is willing to give them.

For example, let's say your company matches your contribution up to 3% of your income. If you make $60,000 per year then you would want to contribute $1,800 ($60,000 X .03) to your employer sponsored plan because your $1,800 contribution would earn you another $1,800 match from your employer. This is free money! Take all of it you can get. However, once you reach the free money threshold, stop contributing and evaluate your next best step.

Each plan is different, so check with your plan administrator to find out what you need to contribute to maximize the free money. But once that level is reached (and it is usually quite small) – stop! Don't put any more money into your tax-qualified account. If you continue to contribute *above* the match level, you will have skipped over the second item on the list (Tax-Free Money) and find yourself at number three (Tax-Deferred Money.)

#2 – Tax-Free Money. The pots of money illustration above shows very clearly what options you have to build tax-free dollars. If your household brings in a hefty income then you really only have one option – life insurance. The nice thing about life insurance, however, is that it can be structured in such a way to work very similarly to a Roth IRA, but without the income limitations. Now please note that it is *not* a Roth IRA; it can simply perform similarly, as I will describe in the next chapter.

If your income threshold is below the phase-out level and you can contribute to a Roth IRA, that too is a very good option. It's at least a potential starting place. "But," you may ask, "if life insurance does the same thing, should I even open up a Roth IRA?" The answer to that is very individualized; it may be "yes;" it may be "no."

The first scenario I want to discuss is one in which an individual has *no need for life insurance and is going to save less than the $4,000 per year* allowed by a Roth IRA. If these are *both* true, then likely a Roth IRA is preferable to life insurance, because the Roth IRA has no internal death-benefit cost associated with it, so every dollar that gets deposited goes directly into the investment portion (minus company fees of course.)

The second scenario in which a Roth IRA might be a preferable choice is for individuals who are close to retirement and may not have enough time before the withdrawal phase to properly fund the life insurance option. Again, the situation is individualized and a qualified life insurance agent should easily be able to walk you through the best option for your specific situation.

#3 – Tax-Deferred Money. I don't need to belabor this point since we have spent so much time in this book discussing the tax-deferred option. Too often people pour money into this category and have skipped over category #2 – *Tax-Free Money* – completely. In my opinion, that is a mistake. Remember, this is *The Smart Money Investment Order*. Be smart!

#4 – Taxable Money. Just about everything else is taxable – money that receives no tax breaks either now or in the future.

There you have it – *The Smart Money Investment Order*.

Let's now explore the second rule of money before we jump into the technical aspects of how life insurance can provide its stellar strategy for long-term accumulation. The second rule of money is this – *Less Tax is Better*. Yes, that does sound very elementary. And it is. But if it is so obvious, then why are most people dumping money into accounts where they will pay *more* tax? Maybe they subscribe to a secret rule of money called, *More Tax is Better*.

To illustrate this rule, I am going to use a series of graphs. These graphs will show pictorially what I have been describing verbally. For starters, please reference figure 18.3 below.

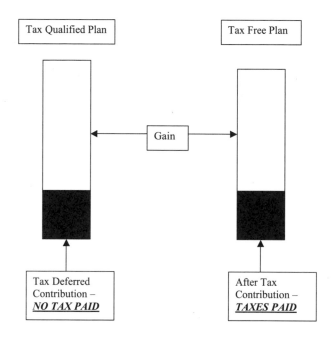

Figure 18.3

The first bar on the left represents a tax-qualified plan, such as a 401(k), 403 (b), or IRA. The shaded part at the bottom of the graph represents the *contribution* that has been put into this account by the participant. As you can see, the majority of money in the account at maturity is *not* the money deposited, but rather the growth on that money – the gain. As the graph shows, there has been *no tax paid on the shaded portion*, the contribution. But upon withdrawal, *the entire account, including the contribution gets 100% fully taxed.*

The second bar represents our tax-free options – life insurance or a Roth IRA. Unlike the shaded portion on the first graph, this shaded portion (contribution amount) is paid in *after-tax dollars*. In other words, tax *has* already been paid on this money. The money was received by you in the form of your paycheck (taxes already taken out) and *then* it was placed into this accumulation vehicle. Just like the tax-qualified plan, most of the money in the account is gain, not contribution. However, ***IF THIS STRATEGY IS USED PROPERLY***, (based on current tax laws as of this writing) *an individual can get all of his money out, <u>contribution **and** gain</u>, without paying a single penny in tax.*

So the simple question. Would you rather pay tax on this?

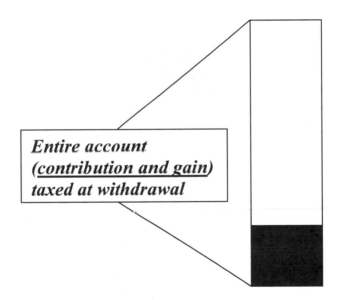

Entire account (<u>contribution and gain</u>) taxed at withdrawal

Or this?

ZERO TAX!

$0 tax paid on entire account at withdrawal since taxes already paid on the contributions

It really is that simple.

** I only address the Roth IRA in this book and not the Roth 401(k) for two reasons: One, it is offered at this time to such a limited number of individuals that it really is not pertinent to most people reading this book. Secondly, though the growth inside of the Roth 401(k) may be tax-free, the government still has enough strings attached that it does not give an individual all the freedom of choice that life insurance offers... at least at the present time.

19

The Retirement Solution – Why Life Insurance?

The time has finally arrived for us to dive in and explore this new investment frontier. All the chapters leading up to this point have had a significant purpose in laying a solid foundation upon which we can build.

You have treaded carefully through some common financial landmines. You have explored the potential tax nightmare of qualified retirement plans. And you clearly understand why a tax-free pot of money is better than a taxable pot of money. I'd say you're all set. Buckle your seat belt and let's go. But as we do, please know that this is the most technical chapter in the book. You might need to slow down your reading pace or read this chapter twice to fully grasp the concept of how life insurance can provide you with a lifetime of tax-free income. However you do it, enjoy – because your financial future will never be the same.

There are many different kinds of permanent life insurance available in the marketplace; but the type of product I believe best allows us to utilize all the benefits of this book is called, Universal

Life Insurance. You've probably heard of it. You may even own it. This is a type of permanent insurance that has been sold by all major life insurance companies since the early 1980s when it first entered the marketplace.

Here's how Universal Life Insurance works. Just like any insurance product, you pay a certain premium and receive a certain amount of death benefit. Traditionally, most agents and companies have calculated the *minimum* premium needed to fund a certain amount of death benefit. This is the manner in which most policies have been sold to the public – the *most* life insurance for the *least* amount of money. This is also the reason that so many life insurance companies have gotten into trouble in recent years. When a policy is funded at the *minimum premium* level, there is often not enough money being put into a policy to keep it alive until maturity, which is usually age 100 or later. Also, in the 1980s, when agents were illustrating interest rate based policies at 12%, 13%, or even 14%, the premiums that were collected were based on *projected* interest rates. As the last two decades have played themselves out, however, interest rates didn't follow these projected targets. The interest rate pendulum swung completely in the other direction, leaving many of these minimum-funded policies gasping for air to stay alive. (As a side note, however, if the agents who originally sold these policies had offered regular reviews with their clients, then these policies could have easily been spared an unnecessary death.)

The back lash of these poor sales strategies, along with this interest rate anomaly, have caused the public to completely dismiss one of the most powerful accumulation strategies ever created. In this situation the proverbial saying came to pass and most Americans (as well as most financial planners), "threw the baby out with the bath water."

Let me illustrate the differences in funding options beginning with what 99% of all life insurance clients choose to pay – the *minimum premium*. If a forty-year old male wanted to purchase $500,000 in life insurance death benefit and pay the *minimum premium* allowed by a company he might expect to pay around $400 per month – give or take. If this forty-year old male continued to make that $400 per month payment he could potentially accumulate a cash value in the policy in the neighborhood of $250,000 at age 67.

If we look down the road a little further to age 85, the cash value could have potentially grown to as much as $600,000. And though this is a substantial sum, it is not the best way to utilize the policy…nor is it very exciting. Who likes buying life insurance? Who enjoys facing the prospect of their own death?

Let's face it. No one enjoys buying life insurance. Many people do it – very often willingly. But do they really enjoy it? No. Why should they? Who likes spending their own money today for someone else to receive a payoff after they are six feet under? That doesn't sound too exciting. I believe most people, even the responsible ones who willingly purchase this valuable protection for their families, see life insurance as simply a necessary evil. In fact, I've had clients use that exact term more times than I can count.

Why do people feel this way about life insurance? The answer is simple. All the focus has been on the benefits provided to the family upon death. However wonderful those death benefits may be, the benefits that life insurance provides *during* a person's lifetime are exponentially more exciting. Like I've mentioned many times in this book, most financial planners and insurance agents are not fully aware of the power of the *living* benefits available.

So let's turn the table 180 degrees and make this fun – a lot more fun. I want you to start by letting go of any previous knowledge you have of life insurance, whether fact or fiction. Clear your mind of those preconceived ideas so you can take a fresh look at a new concept. How would you feel if instead of $400 per month for $500,000 of life insurance you were told it was going to be $1,800 per month? You might cough and sputter. You might say that is way too expensive. You might even laugh, stand up, and walk out the door. (But probably not, since you are likely a polite person.) But, if you had any of those reactions, it would tell me you are still looking through an old, outdated lens; and that lens would be telling you that $1,800 is just too much to pay for only $500,000 in death benefit. What I would tell you is, let's put on a new lens.

When you put $1,800 into any other savings account, do you say to yourself, "You know, that is just way too much to pay for that savings account?" Of course not. Why? Because when you are *saving* money, it's not a purchase. You are simply putting money away, hopefully to grow and provide you with a greater benefit in the future. As a matter of fact, a large monthly outlay for savings purposes is exciting, not depressing. The more you save the more you hope to return in the future. And the longer you have to let it grow, and the more you can put into your account, the more powerfully Mr. Interest can labor for you.

So, if this forty year old male put $1,800 a month into a $500,000 life insurance policy, let's see what it could do for him. Depending on policy variations, at age 67 his cash value could be as high as $1,800,000, with a death benefit of $2,300,000. Not bad. And if he kept contributing to the policy at age 85 there could potentially be a cash value of $8,500,000 and a death benefit of $9,000,000 (original $500,000 death benefit *plus* $8,500,000 cash value). Wow! That's some pot of money. But you might be saying to yourself, "Hold on a minute. If that money is still in the policy, how can it help him?"

Though the money is in the policy, it is still his money to do with as he pleases, just like any other savings account he might possess. However, the largest single factor in utilizing the power of life insurance comes with distribution. Accumulation is easy. Anyone can stuff these things full of money yet not fully realize the powerful tax advantages provided by Uncle Sam to *all* Americans, regardless of income, regardless of age, regardless of any other type of potentially discriminating factors. Would you like to have a completely tax-free retirement? Then read the next pages closely, because they hold the secret.

Okay, so this individual has funded his life insurance to the maximum amount as allowed by the tax laws and he now has this big pot of money just waiting to be utilized. How does he get at it?

One option is, he can simply withdraw it. He can call up the company and let them know he would like to cancel the policy, and they can send him the proceeds in his cash value. If we continue to use the example above, at age 67 the life insurance company would cancel the policy and send him a check for $1,800,000. But he must hold his excitement. They also would send record of that large withdrawal to our friends at the IRS. And guess what? The IRS wants their share of the pie. In this case, he put in $583,200 and drew out $1,800,000 leaving him a net profit of $1,216,800. That net profit would be taxed just like a distribution from an IRA. That doesn't sound like a good option, does it? Indeed, it's not. At a 35% federal tax rate, the slice of pie the IRS would take would be $425,880. So withdrawing money in that fashion is no better than if he had saved money in a tax-qualified plan. As a matter of fact, it would be worse, because life insurance did not provide him with the tax deferral on his original contributions. Okay, so it's clear he doesn't want to go that route. What other option does he have? A beautiful one!

Life insurance companies have set up a provision within their policy features that allow the client to take a loan against their cash value. Not *from* their cash value but *against* their cash value. Your initial reaction might be, "Ouch, that doesn't sound good during my retirement years. I don't want to be taking loans." But what if I told you that this loan charged you little to no interest, and that it *never* needed to be paid back during your lifetime? Does that change the picture? You bet it does. Let's explore exactly how this loan works.

Again, using this same example, $583,200 of his total pot of money consists of his original premium payments into the contract. The tax law regarding life insurance says that as long as he has stayed under the contribution maximum (called the Modified Endowment Contract limit), then the first amount of money withdrawn out of a life insurance policy can come out tax-free, as a *withdrawal* (not a loan), <u>*up to his total contribution amount.*</u>

In this case, the client could withdraw $583,200 without paying any tax. Why? Because these dollars have already been taxed prior to being placed into the contract; they are simply a return of that premium. But, that still leaves him with $1,216,800 to contend with. It's at this point that the *loan provision* gets employed.

Let's assume that at age 67, the total cash value in the policy of $1,800,000 could provide an annual income to this individual of $125,000 every year of his life until age 100. We know that he contributed $583,200 in premium payments to the policy, so that means that he could take *withdrawals* of $125,000 a year for four years tax-free, since that would simply represent a return of the life insurance premium he paid over the last twenty-seven years.

Wait, did you catch the power of what I just said? This individual *contributed* money into this policy for twenty-seven years and he just took it all out in four years. And you know what? In many cases, there is still *more* money in the policy after these four years of withdrawals (at age 71) then there was on the day he started taking the money out at age 67.

And it is at this point that the loan provisions begin. In this example, in the fifth year of withdrawals, this individual would still receive $125,000 tax-free from the life insurance company but it would not come out in the form of a withdrawal from the policy; it would get distributed in the form of a loan from the insurance company itself.

Are loans taxed by the government? No. When you borrowed money to buy your car was the loan taxed? No. The car was taxed but not the loan. When you borrowed money to buy your house was the loan taxed? No. The same is true when a loan is taken from a life insurance company. The individual in this example would receive their $125,000 loan tax-free. Again, zero tax!

But then what happens? The amount that is borrowed does get charged an interest rate, just like any other loan. For illustration sake lets assume that rate is 5%. So, he is now getting charged 5% per year on his loan of $125,000. But, that is only half of the story.

The life insurance company then removes that same exact amount of money out of his cash value and puts it into a separate account that earns 4 ½ to 5%. So let's do the math. He is being charged 5% and he is earning 4 ½ to 5%. What's the net result? He is paying net loan interest somewhere between ½% and 0%. So what does this allow him to do? Through this provision, he is able to continue to access his remaining cash value during his lifetime 100% tax-free with little or no cost to him. It really doesn't get any better than that. Not only that, but since it is distributed as a loan, the withdrawal doesn't even show up on his annual tax return. As far as the IRS is concerned, it's invisible money that he gets to use during his entire lifetime completely tax-free. Like I said, it's a beautiful thing.

The last component you need to understand is how the life insurance death benefit is taxed, because it is the death benefit that makes this whole strategy work. Without the death benefit, neither this strategy nor this book would be in existence.

At death, all the proceeds of a life insurance contract are paid to the beneficiary completely income-tax free. So, during the life of this individual in our illustration, he has withdrawn $125,000 tax-free every year of his life. Let's say that he lives to the age of 87. During those 20 years of withdrawals he has taken out $2,500,000 in total tax-free income. Even if his net interest rate is ½% and he has taken out $2,500,000 in tax-free income during those 20 years, at his death he could have his total loan paid off and *still have an additional $2 million* (depending on the type of policy and options chosen) that would be paid to his named beneficiary – tax-free!

What does this mean? This means a few significant things. First, it means that he was able to live all of his retirement years without Uncle Sam seeing one red cent of his hard-earned money. Second, this means that at his death, the loan will be paid off from a *portion* of the death benefit. And third, after the loan has been paid off, there should still be a significant amount of the death benefit left to be distributed to his beneficiaries (wife, kids, charity, whoever); in this example it could easily be in the neighborhood of an additional $2,000,000 in income-tax-free proceeds that his beneficiaries would still receive *after* his tax-free loan is paid off.

In my world, it just doesn't get any better than that! Tax-free dollars while you're living and tax-free dollars distributed to whomever you choose upon your death.

Right now, you're dying to ask two questions. "Okay, what's the catch?" And, "If this is so good, why isn't everyone doing this?"

To those two great questions I can only tell you there really is no catch. There is a caution that I will cover in a minute, but there is no catch. As long as you understand that you are buying life insurance – this is not like other savings plans – then there really isn't any catch. Most people need the life insurance anyway so purchasing it in this format is a great way to get the life insurance they need and tax benefits they didn't know existed.

Why isn't everyone saving this way?

The primary reason is that most people don't know about it. It is for this reason that I have written this book. It has been far too long that this great benefit has been hidden to mainstream America.

The second reason is that this strategy is not for everybody. Though it is *open* to everybody who can qualify for life insurance, it is best suited for a couple of target groups: those currently contributing to a tax-qualified plan such as a 401(k), SEP, SIMPLE, IRA, etc., those who earn a relatively large income, or those who want to save more than a few thousand dollars a year in a tax-free environment.

In the next section I am going to explore four specific individual applications and why using life insurance for a retirement vehicle is well suited for each one.

But before I jump to these applications, I previously mentioned that there is a caution in this plan that needs to be well heeded. The caution is this. Since it is the tax-free death benefit that makes this strategy work, it is ***imperative*** that the policy stay in force until the insured's death. That may sound pretty basic but it is too important to gloss over. The reason that the policy must stay in force is that if the policy lapses or cancels then all that money you have taken out as a tax-free loan now suddenly becomes taxable; and that is one tax bill you *never* want to see! So, how do you make sure the policy stays in force? Simple.

First, don't take out too much money. When your agent runs income illustrations, make sure that he or she runs them all the way to age 100. Don't let someone try to show you better income projections by running them to only age 90 or 95. And if you think you are going to live past age 100, then take out less than the illustration shows.

Second, review your policy annually with the person who sold it to you. If your policy is returning less than the illustration predicted, then take out less money for a couple of years until it catches up.

And as a side note, make sure you buy this policy through a reputable agent who _**fully**_ understands how this strategy works. Don't buy this type of policy over the Internet or from an 800 number. You need the personal assistance of a qualified individual who will be able to walk you through the best distribution strategy possible.

Really, there is nothing to be scared of. You just need to show caution and discernment as you set up a successful distribution plan for your future.

* The numbers used in this chapter's example (cost, cash value, and death benefit) are fictitious, and represent no particular type of policy, nor any particular company. These numbers are purely intended to introduce a concept and are not to be used for illustration purpose. Any similarities of these numbers to any actual policy are of pure coincidence. Actual policy results can and will vary either positively or negatively based on the company, the type of policy, and the features chosen.

Part V: Individual Applications

20

Tax-Free Retirement for Physicians

In the next four chapters I want to explore specific applications for various groups of individuals who I believe would benefit most from this strategy.

I want to start this section with physicians for a couple of reasons. My first reason is personal. I am the son of a doctor. My father retired seven years ago after practicing medicine in the Northwest for over thirty-five years. He was a great doctor, loved by patients, hospital staff, and peers. And like all doctors, he gave his life to his profession. I am a benefactor in many ways of growing up the son of a physician. I witnessed first-hand the significance of a great work ethic. I realized the importance of knowing your profession well. And most of all, I had the good fortune of growing up around a lot of truly wonderful people. Almost all of our closest friends were families within the medical community. I got to know doctors well. And though I chose not to follow in my father's footsteps, I desire to give something significant back to this community of individuals to whom I owe so much of who I am. Also, as I've walked with my dad through his early years of retirement, the financial picture I have witnessed both for him and for others in this community has been one of my chief reasons for wanting to offer this book to the public.

If my first reason is personal, my second reason is practical. Doctors have many unique qualities. And in my opinion, it is these unique qualities that make this group one of the most significant to benefit from the strategies in this book. In this chapter I want to explore four key realities that make physicians such an appropriately fitting group to maximize the full benefits of this strategy. These four reasons are:

Reason #1 – Many doctors make more than $160,000 per year, which is the phase-out limit for being able to contribute to a Roth IRA. Therefore, they have no tax-free retirement option available to them other than life insurance. And even for those who make less than the phase-out limit, a Roth IRA only allows a few thousand dollars per year for the contribution amount.

Reason #2 – Doctors are specialists. They have given their lives to be the best at what they do – and they are. However, this level of specialty often leaves little time for less urgent activities such as retirement planning.

Reason #3 – Doctors are often taken advantage of by snake-oil salesman in the financial realm hocking half-baked, poorly formed investment strategies promising wonderful returns.

Reason #4 – Doctors generally need a lot of life insurance for three reasons. One, they need to protect a large income for their families. Two, they usually carry high debt. Often this is due to starting out in debt from large medical school bills and low wages during their residency and internship years. Three, doctors as a group have one of the lowest life expectancies of any profession.

That's the overview. I'd now like to look at each one of these in more detail.

Reason #1 – Many doctors make more than $160,000 which is the phase out limit for being able to contribute to a Roth IRA. Therefore, they have no tax-free retirement option available to them other than life insurance. And even for those who make less than the phase out limit, a Roth IRA only allows a few thousand dollars per year for the contribution amount.

Most doctors make a large income. And in my opinion, they deserve every dollar. Very few professionals invest so much, for so long, to provide such a wonderful service to the world. And unlike you and me in other lines of work, doctors can't have a bad day. A bad day can be deadly. That's a lot of pressure. Pressure most of the world chooses not to accept. Pressure that deserves to be well compensated.

And how does our tax system reward these individuals who take on the pressure to keep us all healthy? They penalize them by not allowing them to be able to contribute to one of the only tax-free investments offered to the public – the Roth IRA. And the reason? They make too much money.

However, even if physicians could contribute to a Roth IRA, it would fall far short of providing the necessary income to fund a lifestyle in retirement anywhere close to what they were used to during their working years.

So what options are available to doctors? They, like other high-income earners, can contribute to many of the standard tax-qualified retirement plans. Many medical partnerships and corporations set up their own pension and profit-sharing plans, but these, too, follow the tax rules of the other tax-qualified plans referenced earlier in this book. Also, each one of these plans has contribution caps that can be far lower than is needed to fund a proper retirement, especially if you consider the amount the IRS is going to take upon withdrawal.

The other issue I have seen with doctors is that most of them have few business deductions. They often retain all of the negative aspects of being a business owner, such as long hours, large responsibility, and managing the financial books of a busy medical practice; yet they get few, if any, of the positive financial aspects that most business owners enjoy. I believe that this lack of business deductions is a large reason why doctors pour their money into tax-qualified plans. It's an easy justification. Other than the regular personal deductions (which are also often phased-out due to income level), a tax-qualified plan may be one of the only deductions a doctor can take on his tax return. With the huge tax bill that most physicians face each year, this is too large a carrot to pass up. But again, most have never stopped long enough to evaluate what the decision to fund a tax-qualified plan really means in their later years, once they stop working. It's certainly not something their plan administrator is going to readily share with them – they are paid for assets under management. It's not something the government is going to tell them – they are greedily looking forward to the future taxes. And it's not something the doctor himself has much time to consider – he or she is busy saving people's lives.

Let's pause for a minute and ask ourselves why the government would penalize high-income earners like physicians. It's simple. The government wants doctors to pump billions of dollars into tax-qualified plans, because billions of dollars saved means hundreds of billions (or more) accumulated in the future that the government can get its hands on. And with a potential future tax rate of 50% or more for every dollar withdrawn from those accounts, the government is pretty excited about those tax-qualified plans. As I've asked before, whose retirement are doctors funding – the government's or their own? You have to stop and wonder.

Other than tax-qualified retirement plans, doctors do have other investment alternatives available to them, but most are either too time consuming, such as real estate, or do not provide the needed tax advantages and can create additional annual tax bills.

So from the standpoint of viable investment alternatives available to the physician, we are left with only one option. Luckily, it is one superior option – life insurance! For all the reasons we have discussed in section IV, *The Solution*, life insurance is the single, most beneficial avenue for physicians' long term retirement planning.

It can offer an unlimited contribution potential, all based on the size of the policy. It grows without annual taxation. It takes no time to manage. It provides a huge sum of money to the physician's family in the case of an untimely death. And best of all, if structured properly, all the money can be withdrawn tax-free.

I only wish someone had written this book twenty-five years ago for my father and all the other hard-working doctors that have long since retired. He would have been well served. However, my dad did what most other physicians have done – he socked as much money into his tax-qualified plan as the law would allow. And though my dad's pot of money grew to a rather large sum, he continues to be shocked at the disastrous one-two punch of heavy taxation and no tax deductions, during his retirement years. In a financial sense, he would give anything to be able to withdraw his retirement income tax-free.

Reason #2 – Doctors are specialists. They have given their lives to be the best at what they do – and they are. However, this level of specialty often leaves little time for less urgent activities such as retirement planning.

With the schedules that doctors keep, they just don't have the time to research each opportunity to evaluate the risk-to-reward ratio. Physicians would be best served to stick with a proven strategy, especially one that can eliminate all future tax burdens.

Reason #3 – Doctors are often taken advantage of by snake-oil salesman in the financial realm hocking half-baked, poorly formed investment strategies promising wonderful returns.

It's funny how certain memories linger crystal clear from your childhood. For me, some of those memories are the few failed investment endeavors of my father. Though he never included me in his financial decision making, I watched intently from afar. Limited partnerships gone bad. High-yield junk bonds defaulted. Condos that were held during a recession and then sold too soon. Each one of these apparently legitimate investment opportunities were brought to him from close friends or relatives. Each one promised spectacular returns. Each one failed miserably.

Doctors often get targeted for these types of investments for a variety of reasons. Physicians tend to have a high trust factor. Because they are experts in their respective field, they believe others to be so as well. However, as you know, this is certainly not the case.

Additionally, they generally have enough discretionary money to put some at risk; and those seeking to put together these types of deals frequently take advantage of that knowledge.

Reason #4 – Doctors generally need a lot of life insurance for three reasons. One, they need to protect a large income for their families. Two, they usually carry high debt. Often this is due to starting out in debt from large medical school bills and low wages during their residency and internship years. Three, doctors as a group have one of the lowest life expectancies of any profession.

Doctors of all people should know how important it is to be well protected. They see the devastating reminder every week of what happens to a family when it loses its primary breadwinner. And though doctors, by and large, do a better job than the general public in the arena of protecting themselves, I still find them vastly *underinsured* when it comes to life insurance.

As a general rule, an individual needs between seven to ten times his or her annual income in life insurance to properly protect the family left behind. Obviously, the larger the family and the more extravagant the lifestyle, the greater that figure becomes. I have seen one statistic that suggested the primary bread-winner carry as much as fourteen times his or her annual income in life insurance to be properly protected. Whatever the correct ratio is, I have found one thing to be true – most doctors need more life insurance than they currently have. In the past, this need could hang over them like a financial anchor. But now that you understand this new way to utilize life insurance, you realize that the more life insurance you purchase, the more money you are able to accumulate for retirement.

21

Tax-Free Retirement for Business Owners

I mentioned in the last chapter that part of my motivation for writing this book was to serve the medical community that my father has been a part of for so many wonderful years. Another primary reason for this book was to address the dire needs of small-business owners, who, in my opinion, get hugely underserved in the financial landscape. I know this because I am part of this group of individuals. We are ignored. Forgotten. Left to fend for ourselves. Why is this the case? Easy answer. We are not worth the trouble for most benefit specialists. I have some friends who own an employee benefits company, and they have told me on more than one occasion that it's not worth their time or energy to work with businesses that have less than one hundred employees. Groups of one hundred or more are not much more work than a small group of four, yet the profits to *their* business are vastly different, as you could imagine. So, from a business standpoint their efforts make perfect sense – for *their* bottom line.

However, this lack of pursuit of the small-business owner has left a vacuum in the marketplace. And how does this vacuum manifest itself? Does it surprise you that most small-business owners have set up no type of retirement plan for themselves? Nothing. They know they should. They know time is quickly passing. But they do what we all do – procrastinate. Unfortunately, the future has a way of sneaking up on us like a hungry mountain lion. And many business owners find themselves ready to retire without the financial means to do so.

I believe that there are some specific reasons why it is harder for the small business owner to get started putting money away for retirement than for most other professions.

First, since money is lean in the early years, the business owner doesn't begin a habit of saving right from the start.

Second, small business owners are pursued by no one. They are left to fend for themselves in this financial jungle. Once they are successful, they are pursued, but by that time many are close to retirement with no money saved; or, they are solely dependent upon their business's income, or its subsequent sale, to provide for their retirement income.

Third, the business is hungry. There is always something that is calling for more cash. New employees to grow the business. More marketing. More inventory. New market exploration. Research and development. What often happens is that the owner is the last one on the list to get paid. And when he finally does start getting paid, there is often a list of financial priorities screaming so loudly that retirement's soft whisper never gets heard.

Fourth, similar to the doctor, most business owners start their business by acquiring substantial debt. This debt eats into their profit margins for years before there is enough left over to begin saving.

Fifth, most business owners are so engrossed with starting and running their company that they haven't taken the time to research where they would save money even if they could.

And sixth, many business owners who can and would save money for retirement don't want to use tax-qualified plans because funding a plan for themselves means that they usually need to fund it for their employees as well. This docs not always sit well with business owners, especially in cash starved businesses.

So, how does using life insurance overcome all of these obstacles? Let's find out.

One common thread that was woven through many of the above six reasons is the issue of debt. Small-business owners generally take on substantial debt. And though my next statement is a generalization that I cannot substantiate, I do believe it to be true. The generalization is this: The vast majority of business owners have a family. Does the mix of those two items cause any bells to go off in your head? In mine it certainly does, but I am in the business of risk management. High debt and family dependents spell the need for one thing – life insurance. Obviously, the need for life insurance in this first case has nothing to do with retirement income; but rather it has everything to do with keeping promises to the loved ones left behind.

And while doctors as a whole might be *moderately* underinsured, small business owners in my opinion are usually *grossly* underinsured and in many cases completely *uninsured*. Why? For the same reasons given above – tight cash flow in the business and little attention given to them within the financial community.

So why is life insurance the *perfect retirement solution for business owners?* Let's highlight the reasons before we look in more detail.

Reason #1 – Business owners need life insurance to cover their business debt and to provide for their families if they were to die.

Therefore, owning a life insurance policy is not an *extra,* but rather something that should be a standard part of all business owners' portfolios.

Reason #2 – The business itself usually provides plenty of deductions during the accumulation phase of business owners' lives, so the desire for additional tax deductions such as a tax-qualified plan is often minimized. Conversely, once retired, business owners often find themselves with little or no tax write-offs since the business has been sold – maximizing the desperate need for tax-advantaged income in retirement.

Reason #3 – Since life insurance is not considered a tax-qualified plan according to the IRS, there is *no requirement* for the business owner to fund a similar plan for his or her employees.

Reason #4 – There is no limit as to how much can be saved within a life insurance contract – other than what the contract itself specifies. Since business income can change dramatically over the years, this flexibility can be a big advantage.

Reason #5 – It's simple and easy. There are no separate record keeping or tax forms required. As a matter of fact, Uncle Sam doesn't even know when an individual policy exists. There is *no* reporting requirement.

Reason #6 – It provides instant liquidity (for pennies on the dollar) to the owner's heirs or estate if the owner decides to keep the business until his or her death.

Pretty significant list isn't it? This is all in addition to the already established fact that life insurance provides the most tax-advantaged, low maintenance, fully liquid saving strategy on the planet.

Reason #1 – Business owners need life insurance to cover their business debt and to provide for their families if they were to die. Therefore, owning a life insurance policy is not an extra but rather something that should be a standard part of all business owners' portfolios.

The first reason is pretty self explanatory and we have touched on it in the paragraphs above. Business owners need life insurance. Why? To cover their debts and to allow their families to continue to live an adequate lifestyle if they should die prematurely.

Reason #2 – The business itself usually provides plenty of deductions during the accumulation phase of business owners' lives, so the desire for additional tax deductions such as a tax-qualified plan is often minimized. Conversely, once retired, business owners often find themselves with little or no tax write-offs since the business has been sold – maximizing the desperate need for tax-advantaged income in retirement.

Let's explore the issue of tax write-offs for small business owners. If you're a small business owner, you know that expenses are never a problem. And in your world, expenses equate to tax write-offs. Income *reduction* is not difficult – income *creation* is. As a matter of fact, there are some businesses whose entire profit is gobbled up by expenses. If you are a business owner, you know all too well that you are not in the same boat as the doctor who has a high income and no tax write-offs. Not only are you not in the same boat, you may not even be sailing in the same ocean. Your struggle is just the opposite. Too many expenses and not enough income.

Granted, this is a vast generalization, for I know many wealthy business owners whose income far outpaces that of any physician on the planet. To defer current taxation, many of these successful business owners employ high-powered accountants and attorneys to legitimately design ways within their business to minimize their current personal income. Again, this is simply a deferral technique, not an avoidance technique. And what happens when you defer taxes? You compound taxes, thereby, making them worse.

So, both the successful business owner and the modest business owner share this common thread – reducing current income taxation today is not the highest priority, for that can be done in many other ways. What *is* a top priority is having a flexible savings plan that allows them to dump future profits into, that can be designed to avoid taxation when it counts the most – once the business is sold and/or the expenses have evaporated.

So what does this mean as it relates to life insurance? A perfect fit! As we have discussed, life insurance does not provide tax deductibility for contributions today, but if designed properly, it will provide tax-free income when the business owner needs it the most.

Reason #3 – Since life insurance is not considered a tax-qualified plan according to the IRS, there is no requirement for the business owner to fund a similar plan for his or her employees.

The beauty of life insurance is this – it is *not* a tax-qualified retirement plan as far as the federal government is concerned. Therefore, it does not fall under the regulation of tax-qualified plans; this leaves the business owner himself as the sole determinant of whose retirement gets funded. If an employer wants to put away money for his employees, he can. However, if he is in a position in which he is not able to do so, or doesn't want to, he doesn't have to. The key is this – the business owner has the freedom to choose. There are no funding regulations imposed upon him by the powers-to-be at the federal level. It is completely *his* decision!

If you're a business owner, let me ask you this, "Isn't the power to make your own decisions one of the reasons you went into business for yourself in the first place?"

I thought so.

Reason #4 – There is no limit as to how much can be saved within a life insurance contract – other than what the contract itself specifies. Since business income can change dramatically over the years, this flexibility can be a big advantage.

When a business owner sells his business, what does he do with the proceeds? Great question, isn't it? Most business owners never stop to ask this question because they are running so fast trying to *build* a business they might actually be able to sell one day. But now that I've asked it, let's spend a minute thinking about it. Where can a business owner invest the proceeds from the sale of his or her business that offers a tax-favored status?

Can the money be put into a tax-qualified retirement plan? No. What about a pension or profit-sharing plan? Double no. What about a Roth IRA? Once again, no. Why? Because each of these plans have contribution limits. And if the contribution is not deposited in the current year in which it is offered, then it is lost forever. Therefore, none of the above plans are adequately suited to receive the large sum of money that could arise from the eventual sale of a business.

Once again, however, this is not the case with life insurance. Life insurance not only provides a completely flexible plan in which a business owner can vary deposit amounts from year to year, but it allows the business owner to *make up for previously missed contributions* if cash flow improves in the future. And most importantly, it can be structured to create a bucket big enough to hold some, most, or all of the proceeds from the eventual sale of the business, and allows the business owner to put those sale proceeds to work in a tax-favored manner.

Reason #5 – It's simple and easy. There are no separate record keeping or tax forms required. As a matter of fact, Uncle Sam doesn't even know when an individual policy exists. There is no reporting requirement.

The last thing a business owner needs is more record keeping. Running a business is a full-time job. Think of all the record keeping that comes into play – federal taxes, state taxes, business and occupations tax, employment security, labor and industries, keeping track of inventory, calculating payroll, compiling marketing budgets and sales forecasts, and a million other things to keep track of. The last thing a business owner wants or needs is more record keeping or form filing.

Let me make this simple. If utilized properly, life insurance has no record keeping. That's right – none.

Let's suffice to say that no other reasonable alternative offers anything close to the simplicity of life insurance record keeping requirements. Many other plans are as cumbersome as a bipartisan budget proposal.

So once again, life insurance is a beautiful thing. You have no such reporting requirements. When you retire and begin drawing money out of your life insurance policy, all you need to do is tell the life insurance company how much you want. And since the money is either taken out as a return of the original premium you paid or as a loan, there is *no record keeping and there are no taxes to be paid*. Truly, you receive the best of both worlds. ***Why would you choose any option other than life insurance?***

Reason #6 – It provides instant liquidity (for pennies on the dollar) to the owner's heirs or estate if the owner decides to keep the business until his or her death.

If I told you I would trade you one dollar for every three cents you gave me, would you do it? How many of those trades would you make? What if I said you could make as many trades as you wanted? If you were smart, you would make as many as you could. You'd be giving up pennies and making dollars. Not a bad way to create wealth in very short order.

Welcome to the wonderful world of life insurance. In its most basic terms, it is simply trading pennies for dollars. As a business owner, that sounds pretty good to me.

So maybe your plan as a business owner does not include retirement or selling the business. Instead, your path is one that thousands before you have taken. You plan to draw income from the business until your death and then hand the business down to your sons or daughters. That is a great plan and often works well. There is just one major obstacle in your way. Taxes.

At your death, the value of your individual business interests will be included in your estate; and since it is included in your estate, it will be taxed – and taxed heavily. Most parents who are kind enough to pass the family business down to their sons or daughters are not the type of individuals who want to burden these same children with huge tax bills that can't be paid.

So how can you avoid this taxation? For all intents and purposes you can't. Yes, there are high powered, convoluted ways to pass on business entities to heirs prior to death that can help the taxation picture, but they bring in other complicating factors. And quite frankly, most business do not take the time or money to explore those options. Most business owners die as sole proprietors and the business value is added to their estate. So this would-be-owner son or daughter has to come up with a large amount of cash to pay the taxes so they can take over the family business. Where is this cash going to come from? For most business owners, they have poured their life savings into the equity of the business and have not amassed large amounts of cash to cover this type of need, so the estate is often cash poor and business rich ... that is, unless the business owner has purchased *permanent* life insurance.

The reason that permanent life insurance is so much more appropriate than term life insurance for these circumstances is because many business owners will live longer than a term policy will be in existence. If you outlive the coverage, it does you no good. Not only will you have wasted a lot of money in premium, but you will have nothing to show for it. Not a great combination on the wisdom scale.

So, even if you live a long life and don't plan to use life insurance as a retirement savings vehicle, the need for permanent life insurance as a business owner is still very significant. It's purchasing dollars for pennies; and every business owner likes the sound of that.

22

Tax-Free Retirement for Tax-Qualified Plan Contributors, High-Income Earners (and Everyone Else)

Obviously, individual applications have many commonalities and overlaps. It would have been easy for me to identify six or seven target groups and give each one its own chapter. The danger in this would have become mindless repetition, chapter after chapter of similarities. Doctors have some unique characteristics, business owners have some unique characteristics, but none of these are completely unique to either the doctor or the business owner. More than likely, as you read the last two chapters, you identified with characteristics that resonated in your own life as well.

So the question I faced at this point was, "How could I capture the remaining applications without stretching this section out to six or seven more repetitive chapters to fit each and every individual need?"

I decided that highlighting the primary characteristics in an easy-to-review format was the best solution.

It is my belief that the ideas and principles set forth in this book can benefit just about anyone. And for this reason, my first draft titled this chapter, *Tax-Free Retirement for Everyone Else.* As true as this title may be, I realized that the principles of this book particularly apply to three groups of individuals ....

- Tax-Qualified Plan contributors
- High-income earners making more than $160,000 per year
- Individuals who want to save more than $4000 per year in a tax-favored environment.

If you've gotten to this point in the book, then these three categories should certainly be no surprise. Most of our attention has been given to one of these three groups. Also, if at this point you are not captivated by this new way of saving for your future, then this chapter will do little to move you further in that direction.

However, if you are anxious to explore more and see if this is an avenue that fits well for your dreams and desires, then this chapter may just be what you need as a review to bring some added clarity.

What I'd like you to do is personalize the next section. Get a pen or pencil and get ready to mark up this book. I'd like you to put a check mark next to each of the statements that are true for you. If you find yourself having checked off more than two or three of these boxes, then very likely this is a strategy that can serve you very well.

Do you have your pen ready? Okay, let's go ....

o   I am someone who wants to receive tax-free income during retirement.

o   I am someone who has a need for life insurance.

o   I am someone who wants to save more per year than what a Roth IRA allows. (You better or you might find yourself in for a very short retirement.)

o   I am someone who is currently investing in a tax-qualified plan *above the company matched contribution.*

o   I am someone who is contributing to a deferred compensation plan.

o   I am someone who makes more than $160,000 per year.

o   I am someone who has a desire to multiply my assets for the benefit of something I believe in.

Did you check any boxes? Was it two or more? If so, then the real question is: What do you do next? Here's my suggestion.

You will never know how well this really fits for you until you meet with a reputable and honest insurance agent or advisor who can evaluate your individual needs and then recommend what is best for you – *not* what is best for them. It's very likely that a licensed life insurance agent you already know gave you this book because he or she believes you fit the profile of someone who could benefit greatly from this concept. If you like what you've read, then please take the time to visit with him or her. It may just change the rest of your financial life.

As you choose someone to work with, choose someone who is knowledgeable, who you like, and who you trust. Not only will he or she serve you in the best manner, but the entire discovery process will be a wonderful adventure.

I have had individuals sitting at my desk, eager to give me a lot of money to buy a life insurance policy for wealth accumulation purposes; but, I have had to look them squarely in the eyes and advise them that in their particular situation this was not the best strategy. Could I have sold them the policy? Certainly. They were practically throwing the money at me because of something their friend or relative had told them. But the bottom line is – it wasn't the right fit … *for them.*

I share this story with you simply to say, work with someone who will not be afraid to walk away from the sale, to tell you honestly that something else might fit you better. If you get the sense that you are a round peg trying to be forced through a square hole, then stop, step back, and find another agent or advisor who will put *your* well-being before his or her own pocketbook.

And one caution on this note. Don't be afraid to work with a highly successful agent or advisor. Those who do the best job for others usually end up being the most successful themselves. It's one of those ironic laws of business.

Now, for the other side of the coin. Who may *not* be a good candidate for this type of plan?

o   Someone who has *no* need for life insurance as a death benefit **_AND_** does not desire to save more than a Roth IRA will allow.

o   Someone whose health will not allow him to qualify for life insurance.

o   Someone whose age or health makes the cost of life insurance disproportional to the accumulation benefits.

23

Tax-Free Retirement for Children and Grandchildren

Children and grandchildren? How did they end up in this book? Before I answer that question I need to reveal a little secret – they almost didn't. Shhh. Don't tell anybody.

It was one of those sit-up-bolt-upright-at-two-in-the-morning-experiences. You know, the kind of ah-ha that hits you in the middle of a restless night's sleep. When I realized the mistaken omission, I had to laugh out loud. Sometimes the completely obvious is the most elusive. And this is one obvious application that almost didn't make it to print.

Do you remember the illustration about the penny, or the one about the sale of Manhattan? What do both of these illustrations have in common? The power of time.

In your retirement planning right now, you are dealing with three variables: amount contributed, rate of growth, and TIME. What if you could eliminate the third variable altogether? Well, I guess it can never be truly eliminated, but what if you could minimize it to the point of insignificance? Would you do it? Well, you can. Maybe not for you, but certainly for the generations that follow.

One of the other major downfalls of tax-qualified retirement plans is that they are limited solely to workers. How many three-year-old workers have you seen in the marketplace? For that matter, how many eighteen, nineteen, or twenty-year-olds do you know saving for retirement? Not many, I can assure you.

Do you remember the chart depicting the saving habits of Jill and Mark? Jill contributed $2,000 from age 19 to age 26 and then stopped, while Mark contributed the same annual amount from age 27 to age 65. Who won? Jill. Why? Time.

What would the same chart have looked like if Jill's parents or grandparents would have started saving $2,000 per year for her when she was born? The numbers become mind-numbing. If her parents or grandparents would have saved $2000 per year for eighteen years and then stopped contributions forever, at age 65 she would have an account balance of $8,847,811. Stunning! And this nearly $9 million in assets grew from a total contribution of only $36,000, all contributed before her eighteenth birthday. That accumulation amount is more than eight times greater than Mark's, who contributed more than double that amount ($78,000), over the course of thirty-nine years.

So why life insurance? Aren't there other things that parents and grandparents can invest in for their children and grandchildren?

Yes, but once again the other alternatives face a blizzard of weaknesses and downfalls – regular taxation, massive record keeping, and complicated ownership issues, just to name a few.

There really aren't any great options... except life insurance. In my opinion, life insurance is the *perfect* option.

• It has no age or income requirements for contributions; you can start this for your children or grandchildren the week after they are born and let it accumulate during all those additional decades of their lives.

- It grows without annual taxation; there are no pesky tax bills to be paid.
- The money can be accessed tax-free, if done properly.
- It is incredibly flexible; you decide the payment methods.
- The actual insurance cost is very inexpensive, because it is based on the age of the child.
- You decide when (if ever) to transfer ownership to the child; you can hold it during those tumultuous twenties.
- And best of all, unless your child has some significant health issue when they are born, they should qualify for the insurance; this may not be the case in their adult years if health issues arise.

In my opinion, this could be the greatest gift a parent or grandparent could bestow upon the next generation. Would you like to be remembered for giving your child or grandchild a gift he or she could never duplicate or repay? A gift that will produce a harvest long after you are gone. A gift that will likely foster similar generosity for generations to come. And a gift that could make a difference in the lives of thousands ... if your child or grandchild follows the principles set forth in chapter twenty-five.

Good luck. And happy gift giving.

Part VI: The Next Step

24

Turbo Charging Tax-Free Retirement – *IRA Rescue*

My guess is that you didn't know your IRA needed rescuing. Let me assure you – it does! But the vast majority of people don't know what it needs to be rescued *from*. Any guesses? How about our old friend Uncle Sam. There are many IRA's in people's portfolios that desperately need to be rescued from the tax hatchet.

For a moment I want to divide money into three different categories. Now money. Later money. Never money.

Now money is money that you plan to spend today.

Later money is money that is going to be saved for some time in the future, whether that future is in a few months, a few years, or a few decades

Never money is just that – money that is sitting in some account *never* to be spent. For those of you in the accumulation phase of life, or whose retirement account is under-funded, this may be a hard concept to understand, but you would not believe how common it is. A large number of individuals have money sitting in an account that they never plan to spend. They call it their rainy day account. Their emergency account. Their security fund. Who knows what they call it, but one thing's for sure – they *never* plan to spend it. They'd rather die than touch it. And where do you think a huge portion of this *never money* sits? You guessed it. In IRA's. There's only one problem. The IRS won't allow that money to sit there and never be touched.

Do you remember our discussion about what happens on April 1st the year after you become age 70 ½? The IRS forces you to begin making systematic withdrawals from that IRA account each year. It does seem a bit silly, doesn't it? Having someone tell you that you *have* to spend your money by a certain age. But they ardently enforce it.

But once again, there is a better way – the *IRA Rescue*.

What do you think the purpose is for most people's *never money*? Why would someone want to leave money in an account without touching it until their death? Though people will say it is for a rainy day, or for emergencies, or for a general sense of security, when you dig to the deeper levels you usually find out that it is there to pass on to their heirs. People want to pass something on.

People often think that leaving money in their IRA is a good way to pass on money; but not only is it *not* a good way to pass on money, it is one of the *worst* possible ways to pass on money. Again, as we discussed before, at death an IRA gets taxed as income at the appropriate tax brackets before it gets passed on to the heirs. So, if there is a substantial amount left in an IRA, and the individual lives in a state with a state tax, then nearly 50% (by today's tax rates) can get chopped off the top before the heirs see a penny. And you know my other bias; I believe these tax rates will be even steeper in the future.

Do you think this is really how these individuals want their money distributed? Is that how you want your money distributed? Not a chance.

So once again, let's put the amazing power of life insurance to work along with the incredible benefit of its tax-free payout at death.

Remember, the IRS is going to *force* you to begin taking money from your IRA on April 1st after the year in which you become age 70½. But with the strategy I'm about to show you, that no longer poses a problem. Actually, that mandatory distribution provides you with the power to multiply your IRA in ways you never dreamed of.

If you are an individual who has a *never money* account, and that money is in an IRA, then *please read carefully*. How would you like to multiply the amount of money you pass on to your heirs, and at the same time cut your taxes to zero? Sounds pretty attractive, doesn't it. How can you do it? Let's find out.

You know those frustrating mandatory distributions? What do you think they might be able to be used for? How about annual life insurance premiums? Think about it. You've got to take money out of an account that you really don't want to liquidate. Let's use those distributions to buy an even larger sum of money. Here's how.

Let's say an individual has $50,000 in an IRA that he or she never intends to spend. It's there for security and will never be spent. It's just sitting, growing in value. But once this individual reaches the mandatory distribution age, the IRS says he or she *must* take money out; and not just once, but *every year*. What's usually the largest obstacle that stands in the way of life insurance? The annual premium. What do these mandatory distributions give us? A built-in annual premium. As a matter of fact, the best way to structure this life insurance policy is to calculate the amount of life insurance based upon the amount of income that this *never money* account generates.

And you don't need to stick just to the minimum distribution amount. In many cases, the account may generate a substantial annual income without even dipping into the principle. And this annual income can produce enough money to buy two or three times the value of the IRA account in life insurance. And remember, that large death benefit will be paid to the beneficiaries in *tax-free dollars*.

Now you may be thinking, "That sounds great," but you don't want to give up the access to your money, just in case. Don't worry! If you utilize Universal Life, then much of the money that gets paid into the life insurance policy as annual premiums is still accessible to be withdrawn if an emergency or unforeseen need arises. It's just about the perfect plan.

So by rescuing your IRA, what have you done? You have used the negative aspect of the mandatory distribution to your advantage. You have multiplied the amount of money you will pass on after your death by a significant factor. You still retain full liquidity of your money during your life for the desired security you seek. And lastly, don't forget, you still have the original IRA. Who knows how much will be left in it, and in some respects, who cares? But, even after mandatory distributions, the amount can still be significant. In my world, that is called having your cake and eating it too.

Once again, people are quick to ask, "What's the catch?" And again, I will say, unequivocally, "There is *no* catch!" This is the most sure-fire and significant way to multiply the amount of money a person can pass on to others while utilizing a built-in way to pay for the annual life insurance premiums. This is the perfect option for a person who has money sitting in an account that they want to pass on to the next generation, to charity, or to some other organization upon their death.

25

Leaving a Legacy

I believe every human being wants to know one thing: Will my life make a difference? It's the foundational question we ponder on those occasional sleepless nights. It's a question unique to the human race. Birds don't ask it. Fish don't ask it. Monkeys don't ask it. We want to know: Did I leave my mark? Was my life significant? Did I make a difference in the lives I touched during my time on earth? It's simply the way we were created. We can ignore the question. We can sidestep the question. We can deny the question. But we will never escape the question. It will follow us until our last breath. And that is a good thing, because we were created to make a difference. We were created *on* purpose and *for* a purpose.

But the ironic thing is, life has a funny way of derailing us from our most significant pursuits. Our grandest dreams are replaced with mortgage payments. Our loftiest desires are traded in for the daily grind. And the purity of our youthful convictions are swapped for the messiness of adult life.

But soon enough we reach the twilight years of life. The kids are grown. The mortgage is paid. The career is in the rearview mirror. It is then that our heart dares to speak again. And what does it speak? The same question that has been branded on it since birth. *Did my life make a difference?*

And if we examine our lives too harshly, we can easily beat ourselves up for all the lost opportunities. For the times we were greedy instead of generous. For the times we spoke harshly instead of graciously. For the times we were demanding instead of patient. For the myriad opportunities to make a difference when we did nothing. The wasted years. The forgotten dreams. The unspoken words.

We can actually come to a point in our lives in which we believe that our opportunity to make a difference has left us forever. If you are in this season of life, or know someone in this season of life, take heart. It is *never* too late to make a difference! This chapter is all about making your life count. And you can. No matter how the past has played out, your future can make a significant difference in the lives of thousands. And that is not an exaggeration. You can leave a lasting impact on the world for generations to come.

I have been involved with charities and non-profit organizations for over twenty years. And you know what? There is one common thread linking each of these organizations. Every one of them needs money. Their work is hampered by lack of funding. It's astounding to me to think how much more work could be accomplished in these organizations if the issue of money could be taken off the table. Countless lives would be served. Millions would be fed, clothed, cared for, and ministered to. Money is the great obstacle for every charitable organization in the world. But it doesn't have to be. You see, these organizations' short-falls are not a money problem. They are a heart problem.

In no way do I want this chapter to *guilt* people into giving. No, it is my desire that as people once again embrace the real question of their hearts, that they will be *inspired* to give. That they will look for ways to multiply their wealth for the generations that will follow them. And the exciting thing is, it can be done very simply. You can invest now in such a way as to make a lasting and significant difference in untold lives for decades to come.

In my professional career, it is my hope that I could inspire thousands of individuals to cheerfully give billions of dollars to charity. And that those billions of dollars would feed the hungry, clothe the poor, help the illiterate to read, and minister to the hurting and lonely. And there is not one part of me that believes this is too lofty a goal.

So, do you want to make a difference? Do you want to make your life and your wealth count? You can!

Knowing that this book has centered on the miracle of life insurance, it is no surprise that once again we will employ its powers to create this new vision for our lives. What you have read so far in this book gets you ninety-nine percent there. We are left with just the last critical one percent. And this last one percent *is* critical, for it is not how we begin a race that matters, but rather how we finish that counts.

This reminds me of a true story from the 1968 Olympics. A full hour after the winner of the Olympic marathon had crossed the finish line, Tanzania's John Stephen Akhwari limped across the finish line, injured from a fall early in the race. Asked why he didn't quit, he said, "My country didn't send me 7,000 miles to start the race. My country sent me here to finish the race."[12]

Just like that runner, I believe we all want to finish strong. The first 26 miles of our lives we spend acquiring and accumulating. But then it comes down to the last few yards. The last one percent. And what is that last one percent of our race in a financial sense – *distribution*. What are we going to leave behind and *to whom* are we going to leave it?

For just a moment, pause and ask yourself a question. Really. This is not a rhetorical question. Just pause for a moment and see which of these visions causes your heart to beat just a little faster. When you die, would you rather leave your wealth to your kids so they can buy a nicer car or build a bigger house? Or would you like to designate your wealth in such a way as to become a champion for the less fortunate, to build houses for the homeless, to feed the hungry, to bring hope to the hopeless, knowing that each life you touch will be replicated in other lives touched through the centuries? Doesn't that second scenario give you a renewed sense of significance?

If you utilize life insurance for building a *Tax-Free Retirement* or for performing an *IRA Rescue* as this book describes, you will likely find that there will be an abundance of money still in your policy long after it is needed for your own uses. So what do you do with all this money? Who's going to get all that wealth? Who will you transfer it to?

Without thinking through possible options, many people pass all of it to their children, grandchildren, or other living relatives. And please hear me; there is nothing wrong with passing money to your children or relatives, especially if there are needs that exist in their lives. But for most of us, our kids will have enough. They really don't need any more. Our inheritance will become more troublesome to them then it will be helpful. Trust me. I can't tell you the number of individuals and families I have seen torn apart by the distribution of a parent's wealth. Aren't our family relationships much more important than money? Of course. Not only that, but as we give out of a lofty vision for the hurting of this world, many of our children will follow suit. We can, therefore, not only leave a legacy of money; we can more importantly leave a legacy of the *spirit of giving*.

In reality, some of our things will be passed on to our heirs, but it's not an all-or-nothing proposition. What if part of your money went to an organization that you are currently passionate about? Think how fun that phone call would be. Let's say you are passionate about providing for the needs of the poor in this world. One organization doing great work in that area is World Concern, based out of Seattle, Washington. Let's say this is one of the organizations you choose to leave money to. The conversation might go something like this:

"Hi, could I please speak to the president of World Concern?"

"Sure, just one moment please."

"Hi there. You don't know me, and I wasn't sure who to talk with in your organization, so I decided to start at the top. I love what your organization is doing for the needy and hurting around the world, and I want to assign you 50% of my life insurance policy so that when I die, a portion of my estate will go directly to you."

Silence.

"Hello, are you still there?" you ask.

"Yes, I'm sorry. I've just never had a call quite like this before. I don't know what to say. That is incredibly generous. Thank you."

"It's my pleasure. Thank you for what your organization continues to do around the world. I am proud to give to an organization that makes such a tremendous difference."

"Your words are very kind. Thank you. Before you go, could I ask you a very pragmatic question regarding your gift?"

"Sure. What would you like to know?"

"Obviously, since it is life insurance proceeds, we know that the gift won't be given until some time in the future, but how much might you be thinking about giving?"

"Well, I don't have an exact amount because the total benefit amount will continue to change into the future, but it should be in the neighborhood of three to four million."

Again, silence.

"You're kidding, right? Did I miss something? In all my life I have never had a call quite like this before."

"No. Truly, this isn't a joke. I want my life to make a difference even after I am gone, and I believe that your organization embodies the vision to do just that. Please use the money wisely and make a difference in as many lives as you can. Thank you."

How will that be for your swan song? I can only imagine how much fun that day will be.

How do you do this? It's simple. All you have to do is update your beneficiary form to designate what percentage you want to go to which person or organization. That's it! That's the last one percent of the race. The distribution of our money will be the point in which we cross our financial finish line. And nothing could be simpler than directing life insurance proceeds. There are no high-cost estate legal fees. There are no complicated tax ramifications. There are no lengthy forms to fill out. Just a simple change of beneficiary, and it's done.

As a side note, this vision can be taken to great and exciting lengths using an assortment of different kinds of trusts, but the scope of this chapter is not set up to adequately deal with the complexities of that topic. This chapter is intended to enlarge your vision. To help you answer the question of your heart, "Did my life make a difference?"

My desire is that you *will* be able to answer this question with a resounding, "Yes! My life did make a difference!" Use the power of life insurance to multiply your wealth. And then use that wealth to bring comfort and solace to countless lives that have been cast aside by our world.

Dream big! Make a difference! Leave a legacy!

(Endnotes)

[1] Dominguez, Joe & Rubin, Vicki. Your Money or Your Life. Penguin Books, 1992.

[2] Weldon, Joel H. The Unlimited Times. Joel H. Weldon & Associates, Inc., 1997.

[3] As told in a sermon by Pastor Gino Grunberg, Harbor Christian Center, Gig Harbor, Washington

[4] This idea is credited to Larry Burkett

[5] 2 Corinthians 9:6. The New International Bible.

[6] Social Security Administration. "About Social Security's Future...." Your Social Security Statement. www.socialsecurity.gov, pg 1, col. 1&2.

[7] U.S. National Debt Clock – http://www.brillig.com/debt_clock/

[8] Fram, Alan. "Senate votes to let US borrow up to $8.18 trillion." The Boston Globe. November 18, 2004.

[9] Welna, David. "Congress Sets new Federal Debt limit: $9 Trillion." National Public Radio, Morning Edition. March 16, 2006.

[10] Internal Revenue Service, United States Department of the Treasury. IRS Publication 590 (2005), Individual Retirement Arrangements (IRAs). www.irs.gov/formspubs

[11] Internal Revenue Service, United States Department of the Treasury. 2006 Federal Tax Rate Schedules. www.irs.gov/formspubs

[12] As told in a sermon by Pastor Stuart Bond, Chapel Hill Presbyterian Church, Gig Harbor, Washington